THIRTEEN STEPS
An Empowerment Process for Women

THIRTEEN STEPS
An Empowerment Process for Women

BONITA L. SWAN

spinsters | *aunt lute*

SAN FRANCISCO

First Edition
10-9-8-7-6-5-4-3-2

Spinsters/Aunt Lute Book Company
P.O. Box 410687
San Francisco, CA 94141

Cover Illustration: Kelly Gennert
Cover Text and Design: Pam Wilson Design Studio

Production: Eileen Anderson, Martha Davis, Debra DeBondt, Ellen Doudna, Laura Jiménez, Cindy Lamb, Madeleine Lim, Nicole Livingston, Shelley Salamensky

Printed in the U.S.A.

Library of Congress Cataloging-in-Publication Data
Swan, Bonita Letitia, 1934—
    Thirteen Steps : an empowerment process for women / by Bonita Letitia Swan — 1st ed.
        p .cm.
    ISBN 0-933216-68-8 : $8.95
    1. Co-dependence (Psychology)—Popular works. 2. Women—Psychology. 3. Self-care, Health. I. Title.
RC569.5.C63S93   1989
616.86—d c20   89-35645
                                                                        CIP

Grateful acknowledgment is made for permission to quote from the following: Sue Morrow, "you are my sister." Copyright © 1989 by Sue Morrow. Reprinted by permission of the author. Donna Hawxhurst and Sue Morrow, *Living Our Visions: Building Feminist Community*. Copyright © 1984 by Donna Hawxhurst and Sue Morrow. Reprinted by permission. Connierae Andreas and Steve Andreas, Introduction, in Richard Bandler and John Grinder, *Reframing: Neuro-Linguistic Programming and the Transformation of Meaning*. Copyright © 1982 by Richard Bandler and John Grinder. Reprinted by permission of Real People Press. Laura J. Kehrer, R.N., M.S., C.S., "That Special Oneness." Copyright © 1989 by Laura J. Kehrer. Reprinted by permission. Alice Walker, *Horses Make a Landscape Look More Beautiful*. Copyright © 1986 by Alice Walker. Reprinted by permission of Harcourt Brace Jovanovich. Ralph Blum, *The Book of Runes*. Copyright © 1983 by Ralph Blum. Reprinted by permission of St. Martin's Press, Inc., New York. Vicki Noble, *Motherpeace: A Way to the Goddess Through Myth, Art, and Tarot*. Copyright © 1983 by Vicki Noble. Reprinted by permission of Harper & Row, Publishers, Inc.
    Brief excerpts from the following also appear in the book: Lily Tomlin and Jane Wagner, *In Search of Intelligent Life in the Universe*. Harper & Row, Publishers, Inc., New York, 1986. May Sarton, *At Seventy*. W.W. Norton & Company, Inc., New York, 1984. Meg Christian, *Meg and Chris at Carnegie Hall*. Olivia Records, Oakland, CA, 1983. Kahlil Gibran, from "On Children" in *The Prophet*. Alfred A. Knopf, Inc., New York, 1923, 1951. Adrienne Rich, *On Lies, Secrets, and Silence: Selected Prose 1966-1978*. W.W. Norton & Company, Inc., New York, 1979.

○ Acknowledgments

This book is a reflection of the ideas, concepts, and theories I have read, studied, or heard in conversations over the past forty years.

It is hard to know what is mine, and what belongs to others. I have always had a hunger for knowledge, so I learned early to listen and discover ideas, tucking them away in my mind and heart for safekeeping. Therefore, I have so many people to thank; some are known to me and some are only vague memories. I am grateful to anyone who took the time to touch my life.

Although the members of my family of origin are no longer alive, they are always only a memory away. I am grateful to them for their examples of strength, love, compassion, pride, courage, values, convictions, and life skills that I used to gain understanding and control of my life.

The people in my life *now* are my family, and many of them have encouraged and supported me in publishing this book. Ethel was the first to tell me that the Thirteen Steps had touched *her* life, and if published, would touch the lives of other women. I am grateful to you, Ethel, for your vision and for helping me to stretch mine. I thank Barbara Bigham, the free-lance writer and editor, who never allowed me to turn them over to someone else, encouraging me to develop them myself. I also thank the Women's Studies Program at Arizona State University for graciously giving me computer time, while Dr. Annis Hopkins coaxed it into saying what I wanted it to, in a most gentle and loving manner. Thank you, Annis. You are a beautiful, intelligent, strong, and powerful woman. Working on this book with you has been a joy.

Donna Hawxhurst, author, musician, and therapist, taught me the basics of feminist theory. She did this from a practical and manageable perspective, in such a way that I could integrate it into my life with excitement and painlessly "let go" of outdated ideas that were not working. The many hours I spent in your groups, workshops and office are precious to me. I thank you, Donna, for your encouragement and love.

Sue Morrow, author, poet, therapist, musician, and advocate for women, has also been a support. Her compassion for the pain I've experienced, her unshakeable belief in my ability, her gentle effervescence are rays of sunshine on dreary days and bring healing. Thank you, Sue.

Linda Lee, my close friend, who translated my dictation and longhand into her typewriter (in the *very* beginning), alternating this with trips to the microwave and the teapot—all the while calling me an Author—is my constant support. Thanks Lindy. I love you.

Diane Stein, author and friend, gave me spiritual counsel across the miles, which helped me to understand the energies out in the world designed to "stop me." Your counsel gave me courage, "at the turns in the road," to keep on in spite of the setbacks. Thank you, Diane.

Vicki Noble, author, has written material and conducted workshops that have changed many lives, mine included. Thank you, Vicki.

Lee Lanning, author, poet, and publisher, was a guest in my home, read the Thirteen Steps and encouraged me to contact Spinsters/Aunt Lute. Thank you, Lee, for believing in "Her."

Joan Pinkvoss and Sherry Thomas and *all* the women at Spinsters/Aunt Lute provided the enormous commitment needed for me to "dare to dream" that I could see *my* words in print, let alone have that dream become a reality. "Thank you" seems so inadequate in expressing my gratitude. The process has been tedious and valuable. You will always be special to me.

Then, of course, the courage, risk-taking, journal writing, and growth of my first Thirteen Step group completed the cycle for me. Because of you, Marnie, Jenny, Alice, Lin, Linda and all the rest of you, I know that *my* life experiences and journey can touch and heal. Just like a pebble thrown into a pond, all women's lives *can* "ripple out healing and empowerment." You did it by pushing through the fear and creating a safe, non-judgmental, honest, loving, and affirming space for each of us. Thank you, I love you all.

And finally, to my wonderful children, their partners, and my beautiful grandchildren: I know you are busy being "thirtysomething" or too young to clearly understand just what I have been doing all this time with this book, but I want to thank you for coming into my life and teaching me the things I need to know. I know that someday you will understand this gift I give with love.

Swan

This book is dedicated to my mother whose courage and love made a far more lasting impression on me than anything else between us. She died December 29, 1969

and

to my children's other grandmother who has been mom to me for a long time, and who at age 86 continues to touch the lives of those who love her with her beauty and strength.

you are my sister.

in your journal are words that express your Self and your Spirit.

i pledge to you my respect. i promise i will treat what you have shared with honor and with love. i will do my best to listen with my heart to the pain and joy that makes you unique. i will also do my best to celebrate the ways which i can learn from you, a woman different from me.

i ask for your trust as i give you my respect and love.

you are my sister.

Sue Morrow

○ Introduction

Some years ago, I walked into the office of the director of nursing at a famous psychiatric hospital in the Midwest, to interview for a nursing position. I sat down in front of the large desk, and exchanged introductions with the director. After a short pause, she said, "Are you compulsive?" I answered, "Uh…um…well, what do you mean by compulsive?" She replied, "You know, when you enter a room, for example, a nurses' station, do you have a need to straighten up the desk?" I said, "Uh…um…well, I don't know…I don't think so." I didn't know why she had asked me that question. I knew that nurses' stations *do* get cluttered and someone straightens them, but I still don't know if to be "compulsive" in that context was "good" or "bad." I do know I got the job!

That was the first time I had heard the word *compulsive* in relationship to me and to my behavior. Until that time, compulsivity was a diagnosis given to *other* people, those who were sick and different from me.

During the time that I worked at that hospital, I had many experiences which led me to understand that no one can be so easily categorized. For instance, one day, after morning report, I made rounds, checking on each patient's whereabouts (we did this every half hour). This was my second day of work on this unit and my first encounter with "Mary." Opening the door to her room, I glanced around. The blinds were drawn, the light dim. Mary was sitting in a chair bundled in a blanket, with a sketch pad and pencil in her lap.

I moved slowly toward her, calling her name and introducing myself. She did not respond. I asked, "Are you going to breakfast?" Still no answer. I walked over and after standing near her for a while, I asked, "May I see your drawing?" I moved closer to glance at her drawing much as an adult would with a child, to find a way to connect, not expecting to see what I did. On the sketch pad was a complete scene of a meadow with a mare and a colt beautifully detailed.

I later learned that Mary, diagnosed with an obsessive-compulsive personality disorder, was a talented illustrator and artist, had come to the hospital as a teenager, and now, as a young adult, only sketched when she was depressed. I sadly accepted her as "sick." Mary showed me her strength several months later when a call came that a sibling had been seriously injured and would be paralyzed for life. Two hours after her therapist told her about the accident, she came out of her room attractively dressed with her luggage packed, and filled out a request for a pass. Then she went to the phone and called the airlines for reservations. She stated, "My family needs me—I'm going home to help Mom!" Soon after this family visit, she was dismissed from the hospital (after seven and a half years).

And then there was "Tina," who was diagnosed with "Infantile Personality." Her treatment plan read in bold red ink:

"Ignore patient when she uses baby talk to express herself."

At the time, the staff just laughed when a social worker on holiday break reported that she had seen Tina get out of a cab at the airport, pay the driver, check her bags, get her boarding pass, and go through the scanner, not only in an adult, calm, mature way, but even personably!

I will never forget "Bill," who was admitted for psychosis following heavy use of marijuana. This young man slept all the time, never cleaned his room, went to his activities only when he felt like it, and frankly was an all-around "pain in the neck." His father, a self-made, wealthy rancher, was flying to the hospital several times a month for family therapy. During what turned out to be the last session, Bill's father became fed up.

He tilted his chair back slightly, put his boots up on the desk, folded his arms across his chest, turned toward his son, and stated, "I have paid more than $6000 a month for you to be here and this is what I see: an unshaven, stooped-shouldered, sad-looking person who is learning to depend on a whole lot of people to keep him from smoking dope. I love you, son, I work hard for my money and I give to my family willingly, but I will not spend one more dime on this setup. Six weeks from today, I'll give you rent for six months, a car, and $1000. The rest is up to you."

At 7:15 the next morning, Bill came to the nurses' desk and asked me, "Is jogging a good way to get started in the morning?" I responded, "For some people it is." He went jogging. From then on, Bill was clean-shaven and went to all his activities. By the time he left the hospital, he had a part-time job and was taking a class at the local college. A year later, I met Bill at the Department of Motor Vehicles. I said (kiddingly), "Doing any dope lately?" He laughed and said, "Hell, no. I'd lose my job!" I responded, "And how's the jogging?" He quipped, "Oh, I hated that. I play handball now!"

It was not until several years later that my professional life and my personal life began losing their clear boundaries. They began spinning in my mind, and I had difficulty pigeonholing the people in my life. I became uncertain that my friends, neighbors, family, acquaintances, and patients were really so different from each other or from me! I began wondering if people just get hurt and need healing rather than become diseased.

That's when Mary, Tina, and Bill came to mind. I finally began to understand that our common human bond is choice. I also remembered that day long before in the Nursing Director's office when she had asked me about *my* compulsive behavior. I kept thinking about compulsivity and how it relates to everyone. I could see that for much of my life, I had been like a sponge soaking up bits and pieces of experience and compulsively reacting to them rather than consciously choosing.

Most of my family died while they were in their forties, before I was 35 years old. When my favorite cousin died when we both were 45 years old, I was plunged into a deep, serious, inward search. I had this nagging desire to name my past, understand my present, and define my future. With my youngest son turning eighteen, and having just returned to work after a serious back injury, I was at a major life passage. My personal search was also intensified by my new job working with teenagers in a chemical abuse unit at a general hospital.

I found that an integral part of working with troubled teenagers was the constant inward "testing" they unknowingly required of me. It was refreshing, though sometimes difficult. The real beauty of working with these rebellious children was that they told me the truth and expected the same in return. There I was—looking at my own life right along with them and wondering, "How can I empower these kids, when I'm not sure how I empower myself?"

I could also see that there were serious differences between the experiences of the boys and the girls in our chemical abuse program. The boys were successful at making the recovery program work for them. Since they had been socialized to see masculinity as "all powerful," they welcomed the permission the traditionally based program offered to be less than superhuman and still become men. The program was written by men and offered boys male solutions. They had the added advantage of being comforted by a "God" or

"Higher Power," which, no matter how it was qualified, was assumed to be male.

The girls were not so successful, since they had been socialized to be completely unaware of their own personal power, and were growing up in a society that does not affirm them as females. They very often ended up in the hospital because they were doing what many women do, "acting out" in a self-destructive way to force recognition of their power.

Unfortunately, the societal messages given to both the boys and the girls were false. Boys do not have to be super-human, making all the decisions for everyone in order to be men, and girls do not have to negate their strength and intelligence, deferring to others at their own expense in order to be women. However, men in our society have many more obvious avenues than women do for understanding that these messages are false. Our program philosophy did not clear up the girls' confusion, and I could understand why it was not exactly effective for them.

Thirteen Steps was in her gestation period then, but I did not know that, so I, too, turned to the traditional self-help programs. My knowledge about myself increased, but so did my frustration.

I tried to take what fit and discard what did not fit. This left an enormously painful void. Compulsively, I began explaining the "exceptions" at every meeting, but there seemed to be no allowance for exceptions. Then I began to understand that those statements that fit and those that did not were about *me*...they *were* me! They were the unique essence of my identity, clothed in words. Since there was no room for exceptions, there seemed to be no room for *me*.

I did clearly understand some things about my life:

I am an adult great-granddaughter of an alcoholic.
I am an adult granddaughter of a foodaholic.
I am an adult granddaughter of a workaholic.
I am an adult granddaughter of a sugarholic.
I am an adult daughter of an alcoholic.
I am an adult daughter of a teetotaler.
I am an adult daughter of a chocoholic.
and
I am an adult mom to some pot users and drug abusers.

(Currently, that would be expressed as:
AGGDA, AGDF, AGDW, AGDS, ADA, ADT, ADC, AMPU, and AMDA.)

Simply stated, I am an *adult*. I come from several generations of people who chose compulsive behavior to avoid feelings, and I do the same thing. After I came out of the overwhelming confusion of all of this, and the disappointment of all the programs I had tried, I realized that I was being given male answers for very real female questions. At first, I thought I could just transform them into answers for myself, but, in fact, what I was doing was wading through it all, setting it aside, and creating anew from within.

It does not surprise me that I gave "birth" to an entirely new set of steps that harmonize with the moon and her cycles.

I realized that I am an intelligent woman, with an intact self-esteem. And, in some ways, still not fully understood by me, I draw situations to myself so I can learn important lessons. Indeed, I have much more control over my destiny than I previously understood. I also began to realize that *how* I got to a certain place in my life was far more important than the place itself. I call this *how* my "process."

Thirteen Steps chronicles that process and continues to be a guide in my life. I still experience pain, powerlessness, guilt, and frustration, but because of the Woman I found within, I am empowered. It is my vision that women will use *Thirteen Steps*, individually, with a Thirteen Step sister, and/or in a group. That they will use *Thirteen Steps* as a guide, creating, with their own talents, an ongoing, life-affirming, empowering process, a unique reflection of their own healing, and be able to say along with me:

I am in control of my life; my higher Self is pure and in harmony with the universe and gives me power to choose responsibly. *I* define who I am, where I have been, and where I am going. *I* have room in my day for mistakes. *I* love myself. *I* have fallen in love with the child of the past and nurture the child within. *I* celebrate my strength. Compassionately, *I* share the peace I have experienced by living these steps with all the beautiful, intelligent, strong, and powerful women who will use this book.

With love and womanhood,

Swan

○ Dear Woman Reader:

I was thinking today about the women who came to the first Thirteen Step group and how we created a time and space for our selves (I use *self* to symbolize each woman's individuality). We met almost every week for about thirty weeks and went through the steps twice. The time went so fast, it was hard for me to let the women go. At some point, I think, we were content to just go on forever, so it feels good to me that some of the women are still "going on" once a month. Watching each woman develop her style and her unique contributions, working to maintain a caring, safe, accepting, confidential, non-judgmental space was exciting. It was like seeing the different colored threads of a beautiful tapestry being woven together right before my eyes. During the time with this group, I decided to use the beautiful blank book that my friend Kim had given me and go through my journals and take out entries for each one of the steps. I was glad I had dated each entry, because later I could see my growth. That blank book was the beginning of *Thirteen Steps*.

Marnie, Lin, Linda, Alice, and the other women in the first Thirteen Step group all had very different ways of using the Thirteen Steps, and I am sure you will, too. One woman wrote a great deal in her journal but found it most helpful to talk about the step rather than read aloud what she had written. She also found it helpful to hear what other women had written and (with permission) took notes.

Another woman found it most helpful to list the words in each step, analyze the common meanings for each word, and then move to a more personal application for herself.

The naturalist and birder quite often filtered the step in question through her connection to other living things, while the woman who was just learning about metaphysics came to the steps with that perspective.

One woman who had been through some difficult times recently found the steps a guide for organizing her feelings in a comforting and validating way which she says became a spiritual experience for her. The photographer in our group expressed herself in her photographs as well as in writing.

An interesting outcome of all of these very different styles was that the women freely borrowed from one another, exemplifying the concept of synergy as described in *Living Our Visions: Building Feminist Community* by Donna Hawxhurst and Sue Morrow:

> Each woman's contribution to the group enhances the movement and growth that is available not only to herself, but to every other participant. In this context, each woman's input contributes to every other woman's growth. Collective empowerment is a result of every woman's active participation and of mutual respect for each woman's unique style of contributing.

I was introduced to the idea of journal writing by a person who said, "Don't worry—no one will read it but you!" That's what got me started. I realize, however, that not all of you express your self in written words. I, myself, have difficulty finding words to express feelings, conflicts, and frustration buried deep inside and I find myself making lists of words—usually unrelated and making no sense at first. I also doodle a lot. For a long time I gave no thought to the importance of these notes, until one day I understood that they were my "babbling before talking," "crawling before walking" entries and were most valuable. I now know that any way I express myself is valuable and I as a woman must make an effort to value everything about myself. All of it is part of my process.

Every one of you has a special way of expressing yourself. When you use *Thirteen Steps* as a guide in your healing process, use your very own unique talents, and proudly share what you choose with other women. Move circularly or in a spiral, feeling free to enter wherever you need to and proceed in the order of your choosing. Keep in touch.

Blessed Be,

Swan

In the past five years, many women have given me suggestions about this work. Sometimes when they would "put it to me," honestly and without reservations, I would get frustrated, because I could not find the words to describe my experience. It was their caring persistence that challenged me to stretch, just a little further than I ever thought possible. It gave me courage to articulate my ideas more clearly when I realized that they really wanted to understand. The two most recurring points of concern were Thirteen Step sistering and getting off drugs.

Although *Thirteen Steps* is about my feelings, I am taking this detour to present my best thinking about these issues. I wrote *Thirteen Steps* for *me*; it is my journey to wholeness. After that, I made the choice to share it in book form with other women who choose to use it for their own healing.

First I will clarify my idea of "Thirteen Step sisters." I see them as two or more women who make a commitment to spend special time together to simply listen to each other with "the intensity that most people use when talking" (Jane Wagner/Lily Tomlin). By doing this, they will validate past and present positive change, provide understanding of poor choices, and create an atmosphere where pain and struggle can be expressed but not used as excuses. They will empower each other as each woman takes responsibility for finding her own power through honest sharing and loving listening. This process is not new; women have done this for centuries.

Since the Thirteen Steps are by their nature philosophical, I find it difficult to be concrete about them. However, I will share briefly my thoughts about compulsivity as related to chemical abuse. I define all compulsive behavior as "feelings altering." That includes use of any substance that causes a temporary high or feeling of well-being, followed by a low which requires a repeat dose when the effect wears off. It seems to me that somewhere in the process of abuse a decision is made to avoid or alter one or more feelings.

Nutritional and health research indicates that in civilized societies, these patterns are established and condoned in early childhood by the widespread approval/reward use of sugar products. Many children of all ages, including infants, are maintained on a blood sugar roller coaster.

The commercial value of these sugar products encourages their habitual use. Coupling this information with the ideas geneticists are proposing concerning the influence of genetics on the metabolic system, it seems quite possible that the stage is being set in childhood for the destructive use of alcohol, nicotine, caffeine, and other substances in adulthood. And, of course, there is the impact of family systems as well.

A woman who has no interest in "feelings," for whatever reason, will not give up a compulsive behavior or its substitute as long as it keeps her from feeling.

The heart of *Thirteen Steps*—my challenge—is to take a terrifying leap...a gigantic RISK and learn to recognize, name, and *feel* my feelings and to understand that no one else can take that leap for me, nor decide the timing or degree of that risk.

Chronic compulsive behavior (whatever it is), and years of not learning to deal positively with feelings, will take a toll. That turnaround, that climb up and out of familiar, yet destructive, ways of not dealing with life can be shocking. The seriousness of the self-destructive compulsive behavior, of (chemical) abuse, is evident in our society, in our families, and in our own lives. Very often, when a woman gives up the compulsivity, or recognizes that her life is out of control, or tires of the energy-draining drive to control and manipulate everyone and everything, or finds it increasingly difficult to avoid feelings no matter what she does, she is forced to look more honestly at herself.

What she sees can be a woman in poor health, lacking the skills to deal with her feelings and not understanding how to relate to others in positive, healing ways. However, as she begins to move toward change, as she begins to make choices that are good for her, as she moves away from "energy-grabbing" people and moves toward people who will validate her ability to choose wholeness, as she begins to give up controlling and manipulating others and surrounds herself with people who will not be controlled and manipulated, she will no longer need to react to everything with compulsive patterns directed by fear. She will make conscious choices directed by inner courage.

The woman compulsively using drugs to avoid feelings can start with:

1. Evaluating and recognizing her physical condition, and getting medical or nutritional attention;
2. Recognizing her pattern of avoiding feelings so that she can begin to deal with them, with new friends, in self-help groups, in therapy, or in the hospital if needed;
3. Naming her compulsive behavior, and after her support is firmly in place, ending it, and moving toward more life-affirming choices.

These elements of her process, as well as any others, can take place in any order, or all at once.

I hope this divergence from the personal format of this book will be helpful, especially to women struggling with the life-threatening compulsivity of chemical abuse.

Understanding takes two things:

talking and listening.

When we talk, we open the way for others

into our private thoughts and feelings,

and when we listen,

we step through the door

into another person's point of view.

Talking and listening—

with them come understanding.

And with understanding can come

some of life's most important things—

respect and acceptance and love.

—Anonymous

O

"for ourselves as well"

—Swan

A
THIRTEEN
STEPS
JOURNAL

When I choose
compulsive behavior
to
avoid
my feelings
I
give up control of my
life.

*My higher Self
is
within me,
and
is
the power I use
to
control
my life.*

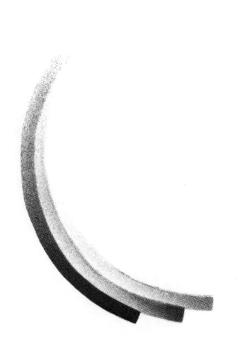

*When I nurture
the
bond between
my
higher Self
and
daily choices,
I
create
energy.*

I
use
warm
healing energy
when I make
an
ethical inventory
of
my life.

*I take
full
responsibility
for
preparing myself
for
change.*

I
openly
admit to
destructive,
non-validating,
self-defeating
behavior.

I
will call to
memory
those people
who have touched
my life
and
name our
true
relationship.

With
"ill will toward none,"
I
affirm,
reclaim,
amend,
or dismiss
past relationships.

*The
experience
of
letting go
brings joy
to
my
woman child.*

*I
marvel at my strength
and
celebrate
Her
everpresence.*

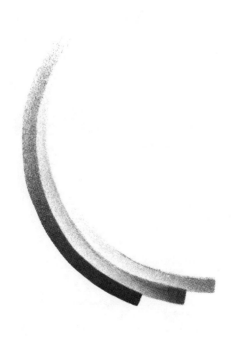

I
make room for the
poor choices
of
this day,
and
move on.

Compassionately,
I
share
the
peace
that
comes from touching
the
woman within.

*All
women are
beautiful,
intelligent,
strong,
and
powerful,
and
that includes me!*

When I choose compulsive behavior to avoid my feelings I give up control of my life.

When women began asking me about the Thirteen Steps, I decided to meet with several of them and get feedback from them on how they would use the steps in their own healing. At our planning meeting, we were very excited. We were also somewhat nervous since we were not sure what we were going to do or what would be expected of us. As an icebreaker to ease some of the anxiety we were feeling, I encouraged each woman to make a special "event" out of choosing the Thirteen Steps journal she would be using at the step meetings and to be prepared to share her story with the group.

At this same meeting, we also discussed how we would use our time together. We decided to meet once a week for three hours. We would take a different step each week, journalize about it during the week, and share our writings with each other at the meetings, being careful to allow every woman to share, or not, at her level of comfort. We decided to start with the step on compulsivity and proceeded as they are written here. However, we also agreed that since the steps are not hierarchical but circular, a group could start with any step and proceed in any order. In the following pages, I will present, as memory permits, parts of our over thirty weeks together. I will also share actual journal entries, as they were originally written by a few group members. This is our gift to all the women who decide to take a similar journey. We send you our healing energy.

Some women had never journalized or been in a group before, so when we met the first time to discuss a step, we did more talking about our fear and confusion than sharing journal entries. The idea of making a special event out of choosing our journals turned out to be a good way of getting to know each other, since each woman's story was so personal and creative. It was clear that we were ready for growthful change, willing to take risks, to trust each other and get started. But as our journal entries will reveal, we were in different places in our lives. Some of us had misgivings about compulsivity, and others were concerned about feelings. All of us had difficulty defining "control." As Alice's very first journal entry so beautifully reflects,

"What is compulsive?
Projection? Scenarios, cannot converse, withdrawn in groups and with new people, eating!
"What is feelings?
Fear, people pleasing, low self esteem!
"What is control?
Being in charge—responsible!"

Later she wrote,

"I must be mindful of the whys behind my behavior. Sometimes compulsive behavior and habit or daily routine can be synonymous. The difference can be seen when the behavior can be interrupted."

The entries by Marnie and Jenny show their journeys, too.

"A phone call at the wrong time, too many beers, unhealthy people or food, spending money just to feel good. Compulsive behavior. Sometimes I can't tell the difference between spontaneity, fun, and compulsiveness. Guilt with compulsiveness. My self says "no" and I do it anyway. I jump first without seeing what's under the surface. No caution. It's important to enjoy and to do it all in moderation, but not to avoid something else, not to unleash a river that quells the stream. I want to control my life, the stream."   (Marnie)

"When I don't know what my feelings are or don't want my feelings known, a protective wall goes up, the acting starts. Be it cheerfulness, sadness, or whatever mood, so I don't have to face my true feelings. I don't like this. I want to be true to myself and to others. In the acting, I lose control over my true feelings. I need to think: why is this? Am I not comfortable with my true feelings?

"I know some of the behavior comes from childhood. However, I'm not blaming anymore. However, it's hard to express true feelings when sometimes I really don't know what they are.

"Therefore, I need to take the time to think, sort, and feel instead of taking the time to act and not feel."   (Jenny)

Lin expresses most of our confusion over the issue of control in our lives.

"Compulsive behavior allows me—keeps me from feeling—to the point where I don't know what I am feeling most of the time. I give up control of my life—to avoid my feelings.

"It has been pointed out to me recently that I have some issues with control—I seem to need to control—everything. Why? Because the opposite of control is out of control? Intellectually I know this isn't true or logical—feelings aren't necessarily logical.

"Taking control of my life includes my feelings. It would seem to be a natural evolution—one step at a time."

Since I had already had experience with the steps, I shared some of my entries from past journals.

"I compulsively see the bad in every situation, and not 'letting go' of it, I almost miss the good, and if I don't miss the good, I don't allow myself to remember it for long."

"I compulsively put so much energy into surviving the crises that happened, may happen, are happening, are certain to happen, I miss the calm all around me."

"A child growing up in an environment where everyone avoids talking about feelings and then explodes over trivia, believes that she must control everyone and everything to prevent the next crisis."

"Not knowing that some things can be controlled and some things cannot makes everything fade into a fog of fear."

After a lengthy discussion concerning our families, I jotted down the following:

"Do not label a situation a crisis on the first call."

This first real meeting was exciting, nerve-wracking, tedious, exhilarating, and confusing, and left us wanting more! We concluded that each woman's process was going to be very different and that we would probably have many more questions than answers.

After the group went on without me, I wrote several more entries in my journal to clarify for myself just how compulsivity plays itself out in my life. I also needed to know what to do about the feelings that I would not be avoiding when I gave up the compulsive behavior.

"Compulsive behavior is so complicated! Because most behavior has worth and is usually harmless.

○ 76

"*Eating* is necessary to sustain life and experiencing the creative ways peoples of the world cook can be exciting. It can be a gourmet delight.

"A glass of *wine* at dinner with a friend or lover is a joy and a fond memory.

"*Drugs* used therapeutically are an adjunct to healing.

"*Kindness, helpfulness*, and *human caring* bathe the souls of the giver and the receiver.

"Productive *work*, 'busyness,' projects, athletic accomplishments are exhilarating, and in our society give us earnings and foster independence.

"And yet:

"If I eat (do not eat) to stuff my feelings...

"If I drink to avoid dealing with a problem I could solve with a clear mind, and a piece of me is missing when the object of my love is missing...

"If I use drugs to alter my feelings, and mind, refusing to experience the fearful downside that comes just before solutions form...

"If I focus on helping, caring for, giving, and being kind to others (especially someone whose life is out of control through her own choice), to avoid dealing with my own feelings, or to gain a sense of worth, self-esteem, approval, or control over others...

"If I work, stay so busy, have so many projects, run so many races, that I cannot hear my body, nor the voices of others around me, that I don't have time for intimacy, and need productivity to prove my worth...and when being proud of what I have done is not enjoyable because I don't believe I deserve it...

"If I spend money on *things*, when I'm looking for love and approval or escape...

Then my behavior is compulsive. When I continue this behavior and think it is my only choice and there is nothing else I can do, I am stuck in what I call 'Dead End Compulsivity' and I am going nowhere. I have given up choice. I am out of control."

With this entry, I realized that my compulsive behavior started at a very early age. As early as age three, I compulsively took care of my frail mother to avoid my feeling of abandonment. As an only child, and to avoid my feelings of loneliness, I compulsively convinced myself that it was better and more loving to *be* a good friend than to *have* a good friend.

Many feelings began to come up when I understood why I was the good, helpful daughter and everyone's friend. That is when I wrote the following:

"All my feelings, good ones and bad, are clothed in anxiety...anxiety is the culprit!

"That uncomfortable feeling in the pit of my stomach that demands a deep breath...it tightens the muscles in the back of my neck, it stirs up fear and is so powerfully familiar.

"It's like the way I felt as a child, when my dad came to our apartment drunk, pounding on the door, while my mother and I sat huddled in the dark hoping he'd go away, or the time my uncle stood at the sideboard in Grandma's kitchen, throwing her dishes one by one against the wall, while Grandma sat sobbing in the corner. Or the time, the many times, that my mother's boyfriend stood behind me, moving me toward the wall, trapping me between him and the wall, moving rhythmically until he 'went soft'...

"When I give up compulsivity and risk feeling, I have to 'disrobe' these feelings of out-dated anxiety.

"It is a rare experience to be able to express my real feelings all the way out to their edges. It opens me to fully hear other perceptions of the same situation.

"When I am privileged to play out my feelings to a trusted friend, when someone listens to my perceptions of an event without judgment or advice...I am then able to see the whole picture rather than parts of the whole. For so much of my life, I've operated on 'parts of the whole.'"

Recently I developed an interest in the ancient concept of "reframing." As I understand it, if I want to change my perceived meaning of a situation, I just put it into another context, or "reframe" it.

Bandler and Grinder's book *Reframing* explains it:

A very old Chinese Taoist story describes a farmer in a poor country village. He was considered very well-to-do, because he owned a horse which he used for plowing and for transportation. One day his horse ran away. All his neighbors exclaimed how terrible this was, but the farmer simply said "Maybe."

A few days later the horse returned and brought two wild horses with it. The neighbors all rejoiced at his good fortune, but the farmer just said "Maybe."

The next day the farmer's son tried to ride one of the wild horses; the horse threw him and broke his leg. The neighbors all offered their sympathy for his misfortune, but the farmer again said "Maybe."

The next week conscription officers came to the village to take young men for the army. They rejected the farmer's son because of his broken leg. When the neighbors told him how lucky he was, the farmer replied "Maybe."

The meaning that any event has depends upon the 'frame' in which we perceive it. When we change the frame, we change the meaning. Having two wild horses is a good thing until it is seen in the context of the son's broken leg. The broken leg seems to be bad in the context of peaceful village life; but in the context of conscription and war, it suddenly becomes good.

This is called reframing: changing the frame in which a person perceives events in order to change the meaning. When the meaning changes, the person's responses and behaviors also change.

In my own life, without realizing it, I have reframed many situations. For example, when I was a child, my mother's apartment was reluctantly cleaned to a comfortable standard when we had company, which was rare. This was frustrating for me because the place was a mess. Trying to get it cleaned up was a hassle even though I really liked having company and a clean apartment. Now, as an adult, I operate a bed and breakfast, and cleaning the house and getting ready for guests is fun, and I get paid for doing it. How many of us get paid for cleaning our own homes?

I wish I had known about reframing when I was a child, when peers called me cross-eyed or four-eyes, but anyway, as an adult, I understand that the baby swan is not a duckling in a pond of ducks, but is a beautiful cygnet in a pond of swans. Maybe sometimes we have to change ponds to see a situation more clearly.

Consciously choosing rather than compulsively reacting definitely requires some thought. It requires a process: I now must *name* my feelings, talk to a trusted friend or counselor, and talk to myself, out loud or in my journals. Current entries reflect my feelings about this process:

"I have not been able to work as a nurse since 1983, due to disc disease and degenerative arthritis of the spine. It still hurts like it was yesterday. I miss being a nurse, I miss the patients, I miss the hospital, I miss early mornings, I miss the 'work chatter' with other nurses, I miss the immediate gratification of knowing I have made a difference in someone's life. I miss socializing, I miss meeting new and interesting people. I miss the feeling of pride when I said, 'I am a nurse.' I've tried to 'reframe' it and see the positive in my life now...and most of the time I do, but when I think of nursing, the tears are still there."

"Today I felt sad and frustrated; an old pattern of allowing my Self to be crushed because someone didn't believe me gripped my gut. The present situation is not an appropriate place for this, since I am dealing with the Worker's Compensation agency and I know that worker's compensation agencies are not supposed to believe anyone!

"Inner conflict takes great energy! Name it, understand it. What is inner and what is outer?

"Inner healing for me is immersing my Self in 'Wholyness.' Realizing that my love, my life, my friends, my doctor, my body, my feelings, my intellect, my behavior, my world, my universe are all interrelated. They are *all* wholly related. They are whole unto themselves and whole unto the universe. Thinking and feeling 'wholy' heals me!

"Outer is institutions like Worker's Compensation. They are designed to focus on minute parts of me and then trivialize that part. When pain resonates through my entire body, I refuse to abort healing by allowing the Worker's Compensation system to make me focus only on 'L_5' and 'S_1.'"

My higher Self is within me, and is the power I use to control my life.

Before we began circling on this step, the group gave some time to evaluating our structure and our process together. We looked at the way we were spending our time with each other each week: circling—each one checking in briefly; then circling again—reading the step and our journal entries; then circling again—commenting on entries and discussing the step, was satisfying to each woman. We decided, after a discussion about it, that at each meeting one of us would make reference to the issues of confidentiality, non-judgment, and acceptance to reinforce our safety.

The concept of Higher Power...Higher Self...God...Goddess...life force...brought up some fascinating discussion. It was clear that we were all in process with this one. Some of us had moved away from the concepts taught in childhood and were reaching for new ones. Some of us were searching for words to describe new-found spiritual experiences. Some of us celebrated a return to old concepts with a renewed understanding. But common throughout our journal entries and discussion at this meeting was that finding our "self"—that individual, unique, living woman—and going within led to finding spiritual power. Finding the spiritual power to manage our lives is connected to that presence within, and for most of us, that presence within is FEMALE. Celebrating our femaleness becomes a spiritual experience. Also common to our understanding was our connection to the earth, nature, and the universe.

The following entries express each woman's process with this step:

"Who or what is my higher self?

"Conscience, inner being, God, contact, voice, self talk, intuition, gut feeling!
  "Is within me (where how)
    subconscious, intuition
  "(define) power: Force, self will
  "I use (how): implement, think about, action, delay, manipulate!
  "To control: act on, contemplate!
  "My life: Learn, grow mentally, grow spiritually, peace, contentment, happiness!"   (Alice)

Alice wrote this the second time around:

"Since my higher self is within me I no longer have to let other people or situations control how my feelings affect me. I can refuse to acknowledge another's power and call on that higher self aided by my higher power to keep hurt and disappointment under control or even out of my life altogether."

"My higher self is within me. However, at times or in situations I choose not to listen to myself, MY INNER VOICE.
  "When I give up my inner voice, I give myself into the control of others and consequently lose my own power of true self.
  "This past week I've tried to listen to my inner voice and to act upon my own feelings, thoughts and decisions, etc.... I've experienced positive and negative responses, but it was MY INNER VOICE. And when I listen to that voice I feel good about myself."   (Jenny)

"It has only been maybe two years at most since I've known her. Used to be conscience, for a while God, sometimes relied on others to put a voice into the empty space that had none. But lately she's distinct, guides my speed and sometimes my actions, if I let her. She's always there. Strong, knows me better than anyone else, and watches out for me full time. Like I don't have to share her with someone else, the poor starving children in Ethiopia, or Belgium. She's me, Ethiopia is not her specialty, I am. I can feel her impatience that I don't listen more often. I want to do my own thing just one more time and she waits til I come back home again. She holds the threads and the answers, she is spiritual. Of the Earth. Birds. Flowers. Water, smiles. A woman. She is sad to see waste. Wants me centered, strong, peacefully relinquishing the need to control, to hold all those rocks from rolling away, the rocks in my arms that I try so hard to hang on to."   (Marnie)

"For years I was burdened with a patriarchal God controlling my life from the almighty heavens. I was raised to believe I had no power except through him.

"I was also raised by an authoritarian parent who taught me to be passive and manipulative in order to cope with life. I had no 'rights' as a child growing up and carried that belief into my adult life.

"I was also an incest victim which furthered my belief that I was worthless, helpless, stupid and hopelessly unhappy.

"It has been really hard to change those beliefs that were carved on the granite of my mind; especially when society continually reinforces them for me.

"Three years ago I was admitted to the hospital for depression. I completely lost hope and the only way I could see out was death. My life was out of control.

"It began a journey that has turned my life inside out. I no longer believe in a fundamental christian religion. I no longer believe I must be 'mommy's good little girl.' I divorced my husband who was controlling and abusive. I enrolled in college as a full-time student. I let go of the major responsibility I once had as the mother of two teenage daughters (I'm still working on that one). And, I now accept myself as a lesbian.

"I think what turned it all around for me was something I learned from a book I was asked to read while I was in the hospital, *Being Your Own Best Friend*. I learned that change comes whether we like it or not and that I have the power within me to make choices about how change will affect my life. I can't always change my environment and certainly not other people, but I can change myself. I made a conscious choice to stop doing those things that make me unhappy and do what makes me happy.

"My higher self is the spiritual power I have within me and I use it to make my life the healthy, happy life I want it to be.

"THE CHOICES ARE MINE…and no matter how scary, I make the choices."   (Linda)

I'd like to share the process I went through to write this step:

"Beginning to look inward, where I was sure there would be a black hole, was terrifying. It was unknown. It was, I thought at the time, foreign. But surprises abounded when I took those first steps, risking finding my Self."

"There's a presence within me that is whole, life-affirming, a microcosm of the wholeness and harmony in the universe."

"When I recognize that 'presence' within, I know I cannot negate my ability to manage my life's affairs without negating the power of the universe."

"'Higher Self' is! It connects me with all that is living!"

"Just as a tiny seed 'manages' the sun, air, water, soil, and other elements to direct its growth, so I manage the elements of my life toward growth."

"Controlling my life has been hard work and draining. Learning to manage the 'elements' of my life to direct my Higher Self toward growth has been validating. Knowing the difference has been tricky!!"

"I thought back today to before I recognized that presence within, to my thirties to the busy days of 'doing everything someone else's way.' Doing for everyone else, the community, the church, the hospital, and the family. My self spent, in *conforming* to *outer*...My Self obscure and unknown.

"A line in May Sarton's book *At Seventy* quoting Mary Barnard in translating Sappho fits for me and says it all:

"'I was a long time groping my way through the fog to get to *Her.*'

"It now seems like a life-time ago."

When I nurture the bond between my higher Self and daily choices, I create energy.

This meeting was short. Several women were out of town or unable to come to the group. Ironically, given the words of this step, the energy level of those women present was low and the excitement of the past two weeks was not as intense. The impact of the work ahead was evident. Yet as the women began seeing the value in the words in their journals, they began recognizing their own power.

We discussed some confusion over trying to work on a step that didn't appear to apply at that point in our lives. It became obvious that *all* these steps are operating to some degree *all* the time. Reading them all every day seemed good and some of us decided to do this.

This week's entries show the mood and process for Alice, Jenny, and Marnie:

"I have had a real hard time with this one. It's been very difficult to get in touch with my higher self these last few days. I've just kept trying to find the key and I can feel it coming together. I am in a bad place emotionally. I seem to be holding my own, though, and that is a direct result of working these 13 steps. I have a good measure of peace and tranquility." (Alice)

"When I listen to my inner voice and follow through on or with what my self believes, I feel a strong, comforting warmth within my self. I need to allow this positive feeling to sink in before I do anything else! Allowing the time for this comforting energy to sink in will help in strengthening, believing and accepting that my opinion does count; no matter what responses it receives. Eventually, this will lead to my healthier self-esteem.

"So with each daily choice, it will be mine and at the end of each day, I can honestly look back and say to myself, 'These were my own feelings, thoughts, beliefs,' and gain strength within myself.

"Allow the positive to sink in before doing anything else!" (Jenny)

"How does it feel to be whole? A circle without gaps, slowly moving, even, measured, smooth, clear, from beginning to beginning and past the beginning again. To be healed, to heal is to continue past the beginning in a circle, over and over again, pulling in the new, making what *is* stronger and firmer, not increasing the speed, only the strength and firmness." (Marnie)

I surmise that every woman has experienced that burst of energy that comes when we decide to do something we just "know" is right for us, when our decisions, our choices, are based on a sense, intuition, that comes from deep within. It reminds me of two statements made by Meg Christian; "Great wisdom from painful experience is an inside job," and "My ship is not on the horizon, it sails within."

Some of the women had a difficult time trusting that power within. I believe it has been purposefully and systematically crushed by social and political systems for centuries. I, too, was not in the habit of believing in myself. I have experienced that burst of energy, that excitement when I am persistent and patient when making a decision. But I have also felt the depletion of energy when I refuse to connect my self with my Self, resulting in putting the decision off or deciding impulsively and spiraling down, down where depression lives. I wrote in my journal:

"I must continually remind myself that the elements I use to create energy are special gifts from the universe. The energy I create is mine to spend. I will make mistakes—we all do. Spending energy on wishing I had done something differently is my choice, keeping in mind that self-recrimination is a waste of these precious gifts. I know that it is an exhilarating experience, a high, to follow my intuition and *decide* for my Self. It flows!!"

*I
use
warm
healing energy
when I make
an
ethical inventory
of
my life.*

This meeting was difficult. Defining *ethics* was hard for the group, especially in relationship to our personal lives and the daily choices of the previous step. We talked a lot, more than we wrote. We talked about everything...but this step. Our avoidance gave evidence of our confusion and frustration. Jenny put into words what she was feeling about this step, some time after we had gone through the steps twice:

"To me this step means: honesty, trust, validation, following my inner voice of what is right or wrong for me, learning from others, validating others' ethics and trying to understand. Trying not to allow judgmental attitudes to be ingrained, to learn, to accept, to gain strength to grow, to listen and to fight oppression of any kind; a strength and warmth."

Linda's entries bring up an interesting thought. Do we truly formulate our "ethic," if ethics is "other," if we do not know or love ourselves? Is love also an "inside job"?

"Off the Planet, Linda!
    Be gentle with yourself.
"It is ethical for me to treat others the way I want to be treated; with respect. It is also ethical to treat myself the same way."

"I was filling out an application the other day and for the first time in my life I did not casually check the box that says 'Caucasian and other.' I felt resentment for those who have always lumped me into that generic category just because

○ 90

my skin is white. It's as if my racial and ethnic background are unimportant because I don't look like a minority. I felt invalidated.

"The question asked me to check my 'predominant' race or ethnic background. The categories were Black, Hispanic, Native American, Caucasian and Other. It flashed through my mind several times—PREDOMINANT.

"I sat back and thought about my rich Native American heritage. My great grandmother was full-blooded Cherokee and I've seen her picture hanging in my grandma's bedroom many times. The question is, 'Why haven't I claimed my people?' Is it because no one in my family talks about the 'black sheep' in the family who married an Indian woman? A racist society called their children 'halfbreeds' and so the shame was felt and the secret was kept.

"Well, I'm not ashamed of who I am. I am Scottish, Irish, German, other, and predominantly Native American. And, I'm tired of being dumped into a generic category for the convenience of others.

"It's painful to finally realize that I've been robbed of the beautiful heritage of my ancestors because of prejudice, discrimination, and expediency. I was never taught about my ancestors because my skin is white. I feel cheated by a racist society.

"And, as I checked the box that said 'Native American,' I realized that it is no longer ethical for me to ignore or deny the beautiful heritage that is mine."

It was near the end of a twenty-four-year marriage in 1976 that I began asking myself questions related to how I met my needs. Somehow I knew that I needed to be more clear about why I treated people the way I did. I also wanted to understand my sense of responsibility toward other members of the human family with whom I share this planet Earth. The most painful but rewarding realization I had at this time was that since I had moved (with marriage) into the middle class, I had not talked about the first eighteen years of my life to anyone, for any reason.

The values (my convictions of what was right and wrong) that I had learned during those eighteen years, growing up poor white in a Chicago housing project and in a household of social activists, had become camouflaged in adulthood as "Christian middle class" values. I had subconsciously accommodated my values to the middle class environment of my marriage, because I knew it was not "okay" to talk about my past. So for all those twenty-four years, most people thought I had had a "normal" middle-class childhood just like everyone else around me.

After the marriage was over, I realized how important those childhood years had been and wanted them to be validated. All those years of silence, learning to be middle class, had been like masquerading. I felt that someone was "gonna find me out." I was at odds with my world, and was often on the defensive. No one judged me and I was loved and appreciated, but I never felt completely "okay" inside, in that place where no one can go but me.

I went back, in my mind, through all those lost years. I reclaimed the hate, fear, fights, beatings, rape, police sirens, verbal trashings, deaths, fun, homemade scooters, trips to 12th Street Beach, watching the fireworks from Soldiers' Field from the rooftop, chats late into the summer nights sitting on the bench in the courtyard with friends; and I learned to unconditionally love the child who had lived it all.

She is with me now; sometimes she speaks through her poor white experience and it is unethical for me to change a word, even if it may isolate me, offend someone, or be completely out of sync with what is currently considered middle class. I now understand the search for and validation of my way of being in the world to be my ethical inventory.

After I accepted the idea that "higher Self" cannot be touched by hate and negativity, that "higher Self" is only influenced by universal harmony and peace, I realized that each time I allow myself to "bond a daily choice" to that higher Self, I create a wonderful, warm, healing energy. It is the very energy needed to sort through the accumulation of behaviors developed over the more than fifty years of my life, keeping the life-affirming ones in celebration and discarding the others. This is the process that led me to write this step about ethics.

Once I asked my uncle, "What's middle class?" He said, "It's about wealth." "I guess we ain't middle class then, right?" He replied, "Everyone thinks they're middle class because they know someone richer and someone poorer than they are." I identify as middle class now, and I am, according to my Uncle Max's philosophy, with one difference. Inside me lives a beautiful street kid whose philosophy of life moves me to look often at who I am and how I treat others. I now understand that it is unethical for me to accept any ideas that are not a part of me and it is unethical for me to deny any part of myself for fear of being left out.

I remember a story my mother told often concerning my first lesson about stealing, at age two. She and her boyfriend and I were walking down the street when we passed an open market. I picked up a few green beans. Mom didn't notice until three or four blocks away. She made me take them back to the market. The boyfriend thought it was ridiculous, but she said, "Next time it may be a diamond ring." I wonder, can a simple incident like this instill a value for life?

I have integrated many values into the fiber of my life now, including some I have learned as an adult, but I did not fully understand these values until after I was able to reclaim those negated first eighteen years of my life. Validating values from both life experiences has been healing, even though sometimes I still feel outcast, silenced and misunderstood.

All the women in the group could relate to the complexities of ethics: those circumstances that appear to have no clear ethical choices, that whatever is decided, someone will be touched in a way never intended, like the nurse who will lose her job if she tells the patient that the "complications" the patient is experiencing are the result of someone's mistake. As a teenager, I faced one of these situations: I was very angry when neighbors would call my mother a drunk when the police brought her home after she had had a grand mal seizure in public somewhere. Yet sometimes I kept information about school activities from her so she would not go, because I was *terrified* she would have a seizure at my school. To me, my needs as a teenager were more important than my mother's desire to go to activities at my school; I made a choice, but was it ethical? That's why it is hard to make sweeping, generalized ethical rules for everyone. Yet it is important that each of us start somewhere.

Framed on the wall in my living room is a poster of one of the women I most admire. On the poster are her words:

> I am the woman
> offering two flowers
> whose roots
> are twin
>
> Justice and Hope
>
> Let us begin.   (Alice Walker)

1937: tagging along behind Mom at her political meetings

1947: growing up on the streets of Chicago's ward one

1957: raising several children in Small Town, USA, in a middle class school teacher's family

1967: driving (the whole family) to Chicago to hear Dr. King speak

1987, '88, '89, '90...: living in the desert, learning to love Mother Earth in this land so foreign to me, opening myself to new healing....

I continue to keep uppermost in my mind where I have been, where I am, and where I am going; I keep uppermost in my mind how I have been, how I am, and how I want to be in the world.

I remind myself daily that I choose where I will live, how I will spend my money, who will be my friends, what will be my politics, and what path I will take to spiritual fulfillment. I also remind myself that as long as our social institutions have some people on top and some people on the bottom, ethical considerations will be difficult and all the more important. I celebrate with everyone who touches my life, analyzing, sharing, and investing in the changes we each experience. Being there for each other with mutual respect, caring, and love, we can make a difference.

Let us begin.

I take
full
responsibility
for
preparing myself
for
change.

After a discussion about check-in taking too much time and taking away from the step we were working on, we decided to each take responsibility to be brief during check-in. If a woman had a serious, pressing problem, we would decide *together* how much time to set aside for her in coordination with her need. This meeting was alive with interaction. The entries all have a common thread: change is inevitable, confusing, and often terrifying.

"No one really can prepare me for change. No matter how hard they try, no matter how much I want them to succeed. In the end that is my job, my task, my responsibility. Changes are necessary, lots of them all through my life, and some can be prepared for. Some don't just happen as the result of a crisis. Learning to swim when thrown into the pool: crisis. Some can happen by thinking about them, by listening to others, and then by opening my soul and trying something new. My responsibility, to look, to choose to allow the change to occur, to initiate it and to guide it along. My responsibility." (Marnie)

"I have become aware of a need to change things in my life. Working on the following:

"Feelings—various group participation and feelings that come up for me

"Attitude—has become less positive. Need to change image and develop more positive attitude in—dress—surroundings—work—activities

"Fun—always had trouble being fun-loving and spontaneous. Need to develop this quality more. Make time for play—practice laughing—dancing

"Intuition—used to be quite intuitive. Have let this fall into disuse over years. Need to develop it. Meditate—read—crystals—metaphysical group

"Responsibility for making these changes is mine. I must initiate the desire and the action to make the changes happen. This entails using quiet meditative time and calling on help from HP, developing supporting groups, setting goals, and making a commitment to achieve results."   (Alice)

"I will take full charge for my own thoughts, feelings, decisions, and my actions.... When I'm old, to me it means character lines from weathering, grace from having lived and wisdom. The wise old woman with character lines around her eyes, who is contented. Looks as if she has learned, cared, and yes, lived. The pottery woman, her hands and eyes so beautiful. Yes, I do take full responsibility for preparing myself for change. I want to be and will be the wise old pottery woman; maybe before I have the beauty of weathering. I do welcome lines of character and wisdom."   (Jenny)

My entries new and old show my need to understand that change that is life-affirming and growthful does not just happen. I prepare myself, even for those changes I appear to have no control over. I will respond out of either *old patterns* or *present choices*. So *now* I assess my reactions to situations by asking a quick question. Is this an O.P. or a P.C.? I know I did not fully understand this when I wrote the following:

"I have an affinity for crisis and seeing the negative in everything. I don't want to be Pollyanna, but I will write one 'good' thing about each situation I encounter, to jar that old pattern."

"I will name my participation in the events of my life and how I draw certain energies to me."

"Do I want to change? Do I fear success or failure?"

"To prepare myself for change, I must 'disrobe' all the feelings clothed in the anxiety of my childhood."

"I cannot carry labels like CODA and ACA and 'let go of' the past; understanding these concepts and dynamics is invaluable to prepare me for change, but I cannot see myself as diseased by them and have them dictate a way of life for me."

Jenny presented the most dramatic example of the need for preparation for change and how terrifying that can be. I asked her to write about this experience for the book:

"I remember on June 10, 1988, there was another explosion of anger in my family. This time, however, it was different. I realized that I needed to search and find a group. A group that dealt with issues concerning true communication, not mixed communication, validation versus non-validation, trust versus non-trust, and respect versus criticism.

"Anyway, after a couple days went by of me questioning myself, questioning why this or that, what did I do, what didn't I do, and talking my Aunt's ears off, I called a friend who told me that a woman named Swan had started a group dealing with issues concerning women and to give her a call. I remember that call. I had never been in a group. Scared and trembling inside, I made that call. The group had already started. However, she was willing to ask the other women if the group would consider another woman. The night rolled around when I was to go to the group. My body was trembling inside. I started getting ready at least two hours in advance. I had talked with my Aunt. She respects me and me her, and she's one I truly can talk with without being told what I should do. Also, that day I had read a poem titled 'Risks,' by an unknown author. It's a beautiful poem and one does need to take risks to live. I kept reading and reading this poem up until it was time to leave. The answer was plain and clear. I wanted to help myself.

"Walking into a home that wasn't mine, scared and nervous and receiving warmth and comfort and understanding. This feeling from each of these women is something I won't ever forget.

"However, being the first group I had ever attended, when it was my turn to talk, my voice was quivering. It was obvious I was a bundle of nerves. I can remember my voice sounding like a wire was loose or half connected when music is to be heard clearly. It was clear, then cut, then clear again. Also, I remember the palms of my hands so moist and my hands shaking. My stomach was in a knot so tight. And breathing was almost not there, shallow and not deep. I stopped talking; I took a long deep breath and told everyone I was scared and extremely nervous just to be there. I was comforted by each woman in the group. You see, it's frightening to gather yourself up, get enough courage and strength and then…then actually meet these people, whom you know in your mind and heart care and who are also there to help themselves. Like I said earlier, I will never forget these women.

"We sat in a circle, the energy bouncing and the strength around the room was beautiful, explaining and caring about each other. When we all were there it seemed as if the room was alive. Our energies seemed to bounce, flow, and smoothly reach the inner circle, the point in the middle of each of us. We are all growing and learning."

I openly admit to destructive, non-validating, self-defeating behavior. It seems common for women to blame others for their situation; it is even more common for them to blame themselves and then sink into a mire of guilt and self-hatred where there seems to be no hope. It is also not unusual for women to turn on themselves out of the frustration and pain which comes from being female in a sexist society. This week's entries reflected the contradiction in our lives as women.

"This step is bothering me. I know I do destructive, non-validating, self-defeating behaviors. I don't like to even validate this. This step stands out or should I say jumps out from the page and tears at me. But here goes.

"Destructive—smoking—I'm a nurse. I see what the hell it does: *kills*, is *addictive*, and *stinks*. Why don't I want to breathe? Am I this destructive to my inner woman child? The one that was molested? Yes, the one, the child that was so innocent and trusting. The one that was molested doesn't want to breathe. I didn't breathe much while I was being violated. One doesn't when one is being tormented and in horrible pain. Physically or emotionally—both. God damn you H.R. Before you took my child innocence away I used to be a happy person. I played by myself, inventing guitars and musical instruments, swinging in the hay loft on Napier Road (which I wasn't supposed to be doing). But I felt comfort in that hay loft, up in the hay loft, yes comfort: 'Stinky' the cat and her kittens and the sun filtering in through the cracks of the barn's ceiling. The sunlight used to shine so brightly through the cracks that the hay seemed golden and would glow. The sunlight used to warm me up and also used to hit my hair and shine. I remember one day, lying in a pile of hay with the sunlight streaming down and the dust particles floating all around so quiet, comforting, so peaceful, to watch dust particles floating by. Anyway, this step triggered for me the need to search and to find help for this innocent child that still does exist within the adult Jenny. I'm currently getting help and feel comfort and am building trust. This step I will be working on for awhile, but in my heart I am a survivor and will become healthy and connected."   (Jenny)

"Lately it seems I've been my most consistent enemy. Choosing to feel negative, choosing to believe in the deeper meaning of someone's otherwise harmless comment, and even beginning to believe there is nothing I can do to change my world. I have slipped back into this again and try to remember how I got out of it before. Chose to really listen, chose to exercise, to be good to myself, have good women around me, draw limits and tell people when they had crossed them. The worlds didn't disintegrate with that one and I felt better. I am too afraid now of conflict. Want them all to like me and they won't anyway. Then I just end up not liking myself. Integrity. Need to get that one back. Glad it's only 6 a.m., not 7. Can still iron, open the doors, feel the breeze and the warm morning light, do some yoga, pay some bills. The evenings go so fast sometimes with chores, need to set time aside for myself again." (Marnie)

"Going back to significant other without setting boundaries or having clear understanding of expectations.

"Accepting others' opinions and negating my own.

"Suggestion made to make a list of qualities wanted in an S.O. Could not accomplish. I must first have a clear understanding of who I am and what I want in terms of myself. I must work first to get clear on myself.

"I must always remember 'I AM A WORTHWHILE PERSON.'

"Driving—too irritable. Quick to temper. Very destructive to other facets of personality that are becoming aligned to peace and acceptance. A real struggle.

"TV watching—once turned on can't seem to turn it off. Wastes my time and energy and is very negative. Trying to tape all significant programs and just viewing taped programs. Also able to save time with fast forwarding commercials.

"Made list of long and short term life goals. Made list of my blessings.

"Lethargy—need to use time more effectively.

"Laziness—need to clean house.

"Keeping too busy—need to take time to know and go within myself."   (Alice)

"Set your Rudder!

"Just because someone chooses to 'punish' you, doesn't mean you have to feel punished.

"I make excuses.

"I panic, when I can't always control it."   (Linda)

I heard somewhere that depression is anger turned in on one's self.

I was very depressed when I wrote these entries. I was still not clear about my anger. I was still acting out of self-defeating fear:

"I continually panic, when an event looks like I can't control it."

"When will I learn that usually when something goes wrong, it has some positive outcome, a lesson I would not have learned if I had been able to 'control' it."

"It is common for me as a woman socialized in this society to feel guilt. It is self-destructive to act out of that guilt."

"I have a painful need to defend or explain myself all the time. I think that comes from always thinking I would break some family rule and express my feelings and it wouldn't be okay."

Studying family jokes tells a lot about the denial in my family and how destructive that was for me:

"Grandma and Mom drink coffee once a day—they start in the morning and stop at night.

"Mom would steal for a chocolate bar. She loves chocolate ice cream with chocolate syrup, chocolate chips, and a chocolate milk chaser.

"When I was a child, I drank half of the Hershey syrup can at a time, right out of the fridge, but Mom criticized the neighbors' son for drinking some beer from his dad's bottle.

"I think all the women in my family had hypothyroidism (my daughter and I do), but what came first—the faulty thyroid or the sugar roller coaster?

"Grandma ate a sugar cube with each sip of coffee and then told me not to eat too much candy or I'd get sugar diabetes."

It is destructive for me to make jokes about my compulsive craving for sugar.

It is also destructive for me not to question authority, even in the church:

"'God' (male) and 'Devil' (male) are products of Christianity. I can't have either on my path to finding the universal force within. I can't relate to what is 'male' at that depth, because there I am female."

"The past is filled with not being good enough, not being approved of, fearing 'an evil force' outside of me capturing me."

I finally turned my anger around. Hurrah for me!

"It is finally clear to me. I live in a War Zone! To be female on the planet Earth is to be devalued; to be less than—I do know, however, that even though the outer world chooses not to validate or celebrate me, to rejoice in who I am, I must do so!! To do otherwise is to participate in my own destruction...each time I do not value my Self I collude with the destructive forces all around me. When I reach through the fog of Women-hating, to the universe, back in time to my ancient memory, *I* am validated. I *am* validated. I am *validated.* I am. I am. I am."

The women in the group discussed co-dependency often; it probably came up in our discussion every week. However, since "co-dependency" is often interpreted in negative terms, it came up again with this step as one of our destructive behaviors. We talked a lot about the co-dependency in our families and in our current relationships. I don't think we came to any common understanding about it, but at that point I do believe we each understood it to be something negative and destructive. Recently I read the following refreshing article on the subject written by a former co-worker that gave me a new perspective.

It happens when we fall in 'love,' lose ourselves for a moment in the beauty of a sunset, are touched and 'feel' another's pain as if it were our own. A Gestalt therapist would call this confluence. Confluence means letting go of our own boundaries and merging for a time with someone, or something else. It is not in itself a bad situation even though in popular terms this phenomenon has been labeled co-dependency, and many are examining their lives in an attempt to eliminate or at least modify its presence in their existence.

It is not our confluent behavior which needs elimination. I believe we need to let ourselves become more aware that giving up ourselves (our need, boundaries, priorities) is a *choice* we make. If we know going to graduate school (or calling a friend or choosing a certain religion or relationship) will mean we need to give up some of our own boundaries for a time and we truly choose this, then this confluence (or co-dependence) will not necessarily cause us difficulty. Knowing that it is a choice means we also know we are free to say 'no, that doesn't fit for me, my preference would be to do this.'

It is this element of awareness and choice which creates difficulty. It is hard to see what our individual preferences might be. Many do not have the support of others in acting on this awareness and choice. Society encourages us to blend in and be like the rest of the group, e.g., yuppies...or politically correct feminists.

How do you recognize if you are confluent? How do you decide if this is a situation you are comfortable with? Confluence can be destructive if:

1. You do not even know what your individual preferences are.
2. If you are choosing to be confluent in all aspects of your life and have no place where your own uniqueness, strengths and weaknesses are acceptable.
3. If someone is forcing you in some way to ignore your individual wants and needs (this technically is not called confluence; it is called abuse).

Take a moment to look at the various areas of your life. See how many of them require that you submerge many of your own wants, needs and preferences.

I began this article by expressing that confluence was not inherently bad. I want to remind you of this. An ability to be confluent…to empathize, to blend, provides a wonderful counter to striving toward individuality and uniqueness. It supports lasting relationships. On a pragmatic level, it is what keeps us willing to stop at stop lights (if left to our individual choice and preference, we might have a very different traffic pattern!!). Done with awareness, moments of confluence are great. When done unawares, it keeps us from experiencing the fullest sense of who we, as individuals, are. (Laura J. Kehrer, R.N., M.S., C.S.)

I will call to memory those people who have touched my life and name our true relationship.

The women in the group had anticipated the emotionality of this step. At this meeting, there was laughter and pain. Each story jarred memories of another person or event in our lives. We talked a lot.

For me, taking charge and naming my relationships from my own perspective is a freeing experience. It appeared to be the same for the other women.

"There are so many! I need to list them all. More than that, I need to examine all the good growth experiences and get in touch with remembering that growth. I forget the good time. Especially when I am going thru a sad or difficult time. Then the remembering gets lost. I need to really acknowledge all the good things. My family for instance. Although they were dysfunctional, they were supportive and nurturing in many ways. I really need to get in touch with that side. A litany of dysfunction and identification that goes with problem areas can tend to rend apart. Sometimes this rending affects the good as well and drives wedges between relationships. Case in point is my relationship with my mother. She doesn't understand the distance I've put between us. I need to put more closeness there, stepfather or not." (Alice)

"When I first read this statement, I began to question what my TRUE relationship is or was with all those significant people who have touched my life. Does that mean my mother isn't truly my mother because she acts more like a child these days? I don't think so.

"My ex-husband always wanted a substitute for his mother but he treated me like a helpless little girl who needed protecting." (Linda)

Taking charge of and naming childhood memories, as in the following entries, empowers me in the present:

"When I was 5 years old, my dear grandmother rode the train all the way to Chicago (150 miles) in a housedress and never made me feel guilty because even though I was supposed to get on the train at Grandma's town and get off at Union Station where mom would meet me…she understood that I was only 5 and afraid."

"I call to memory my grandmother, who *never* forgot to connect with me—even though we were miles apart, and I name her as the person who taught me about love."

"I call to memory my mother, whose compulsive behavior made her the child and me the adult, and I name our reversed relationship."

Spinoza said, "If you want the present to be different than the past, study the past." It is increasingly clear to me that if while studying the past, I find my perceptions distorted or out of sync, then I am operating with inaccurate information. Somehow, parts of the whole are missing. I must then talk to others involved and get as much information as possible. Naming the past through my own perspective after filling in the missing information strengthens my confidence in the present.

The following entries led up to the writing of this step.

"I know best, I give myself permission to name what *really* happened to me; who I loved and who I hated in my childhood will no longer be dictated by the 'shoulds' and 'should nots.' The fact is I know best! I no longer will 'should' on myself."

"I call to memory my third grade teacher, Mrs. Wenz, who gave me special attention because I couldn't read, and I name how much I loved her."

"I call to memory my mother's boyfriend, Gust (who I used to call stepfather), who sexually molested me for many years, and I name him as the person who taught me about hate."

The experience of motherhood and grandmother-hood expanded my emotions (joy, excitement, pain, frustration, stress, healing, injury, etc.) more than any other experience in my life, excluding, maybe, my first love lost. One day while I watched my oldest daughter and her daughter at play, I allowed myself to consider our connection, and the meaning of "life's longing for itself" (Kahlil Gibran) welled up in my heart.

After one of those special intense mother/daughter talks, I wrote the following to my second daughter. It reflects a large part of my life that I experienced without examination or very clear information to make my choices. Nevertheless, I have never regretted these choices; it was a time in my life when my intuition was fine-tuned, but I did not know what to call it.

Notes on Motherhood

I was 23 and had no information about

Motherhood

at least not in the sense of knowing

just how to tell you about being a

Woman.

When you were born, I didn't think of myself

as a Woman!

I was a daughter (first)

    of a "troubled" mother and absent father,

      and then

              a wife, to your Dad

I never thought about what it meant to be a

    Woman

    let alone give birth to one!

I think I'm glad I didn't

    I would have been frightened to death!

      I was calmly naive,

I just wanted to cuddle you, love you, play with you

    and have you love me back.

I thought that (LOVE, that is) would take care

      of everything.

You see, up to then I had done my

      job (as a wife) just right.

    I had your brother (a SON!)

    I had your sister (a DAUGHTER!)

So when you came along, some of the expectations

    were lifted

I was free to have a "baby" since we already

    had the

      "Million Dollar Family"

The fact that you were female

    gave me an "awakening" joy, (all my own)

        I never thought much about what I wanted

            for you to have

I knew I wanted you to be safe!

    (No tension from touchy, aggressive, rude

    men, no janitors molesting you in dark

    basement corners of a city housing project, no

    rape at 11, no wondering who your father was

    and why you never met him

        No fear for your life

            as you moved through your daily task of

                growing up—)

I knew I wanted you to have—Freedom to grow,

    make mistakes, believe in yourself

        and keep moving in

    directions you chose freely;

I knew I wanted you to love people

    and to understand the importance

        of "hangin' in there"

    with a person with whom you use the word LOVE.

I knew I didn't want to mistake "smother"

        for "mother."

So in the midst of the *oppressive* world of

"Wifery"

and the conflict of my own emerging Womanhood

I let you go, to choose, to grope, to fly,

yes, even to hurt

So that somehow your journey to Womanhood

would not be as long and confusing as mine.

Your only umbilical? never to be cut?

"my love."

You see, daughter, I was initiated from "slum"

to "middle class"

in two minutes with two words

"I DO!"

I had no preparation or knowledge

of what was expected of me, my peers had

years of "training"

I learned along the way

(always running behind)

Yet

I never had to "unlearn"

the trappings of that world, when I came

to understand my need to find my centeredness

as a Woman!

And now that I have embraced my Womanhood

and you are fully grown?

We have the opportunity, as Adrienne Rich says,

for "an honorable human relationship."

My truths are herein written

what will you share with me?

July 26, 1984

I found some painful and difficult entries in old journals. They show my remembering of people who intruded into my life, or losses that were "crazy-making" at the time.

"A note to a rapist.
You entered...like access to me was your right!
You exited...like violating me was all in a day's work
You entered and exited and penetrated my innocence
And because of you at that moment I was no longer a child
and yet somehow I will always be 11."

"Charlene was 13. She was my best friend. Her father wore a skullcap and her parents spoke with an accent I had never heard before. They were always nice to me. I learned to like lox and bagels and gefilte fish at Charlene's house. I liked their house. There was a sense of family unfamiliar to me since most of my friends came from one-parent homes, with mostly mothers, except for Mildred, whose mother died when she was 9. She kept house for her aging father and 2 brothers.

"Charlene and I had a fight one day while roller skating on Grenshaw Street. I don't remember what we were fighting about, but she said, angrily, 'If you don't want to be my friend anymore, well don't!' I responded, just as angrily, 'Well, I don't,' and skated away.

○ 113

"The next day at school, Charlene was not in her seat. I learned later that her skate had caught in the streetcar track and she fell up against the streetcar, hitting her head. She managed to get home, but later she developed a severe headache and died in a taxi on the way to the hospital. I completely avoided that degree of anger for 30 years. This is probably where I began turning anger inward, because I believed that my anger had killed my best friend."

The most interesting pattern that began to develop in our meetings was that we talked a lot about our past and present intimate relationships, but few of us ever read those words written down in our journals about intimacy and I am sure there are many.

What follows here is part of a poem I wrote after an intimate relationship painfully died:

"...Those endless moments of panic

When our connectedness faded

and the dark void of separation

made the death of our relating so final...

We wanted to feel the healing

relief of trust in our yet unknown future.

We thought our love counted for something;

But it was not to be, the excruciating pain made "letting

go" seem sane.

You soften your grief with indifference and doubts about

my love for you.

I soften my grief by clinging to that love for my

healing."

With
"ill will toward none,"
I
affirm,
reclaim,
amend,
or dismiss
past relationships.

When the group finished this meeting, we had shared eight of the steps, more than one half. By this time, two women had left the group for personal reasons and one woman had joined late and stayed for about three weeks. Another woman came to only one meeting. We had mixed feelings of sadness and rejection about women leaving. We also had reservations about new women starting with us at this point, so we decided to make each choice by consensus and on an individual basis. We were clear as a group about what we wanted, which let a newcomer be free to decide if this would work for her, and because we were clear, her decision seemed to fit the group's needs. Things have a way of working out if we are honest with each other and clear about our feelings. There seems to be a natural flow.

This step is about our relationship to our feelings; amending, affirming, reclaiming, and even dismissing, are tools we use in organizing and prioritizing our feelings, thus making them more manageable, as Jenny describes:

"I'm still working on this step. The 'ill will towards none' bothers me because I'm not ready yet to have 'no ill will' towards H.R. However, I do believe it is possible to have no ill will towards others.

"My family, I don't blame anymore. I'm trying to understand them and most of my family members are trying to understand me. My aunt, I love—I'm a person to her, she respects me and I love her for her courage towards a lot of things.

"My past lover, I'm trying to heal from. I will heal. We both knew it was time to let go of each other. Healing takes time."

We all liked the simplicity of Marnie's style with this step:

"Diane, amend, affirm, reclaim
Mom, affirm
Nancy, my sister, wait and see
Dad, affirm
Jane, dismiss
health, affirm
panic, dismiss
Jana, affirm
Marcia, affirm
Yoga, reclaim
garden, affirm
home, affirm
anger, amend."

Linda's entry shows painful resolution:

"Mom: Of all the people in my life, I had the most difficulty letting go of her control in my life. I learned from her to be a rigid disciplinarian, a master manipulator, a perfectionist. I learned that I *always* had to be in control of the people around me, and of myself (especially my feelings). At the same time, I learned that I was powerless, so I became passively aggressive. I felt responsible for her happiness.

"When I let go of being responsible for her and accepted responsibility for my own life, I began to feel like an adult. I still see her as a terrified child who survives the best way she knows how and I love her just the way she is without taking responsibility for her happiness (or lack of it).

"Grandpa: This man I called grandpa was a dark shadow that haunted my life for many years. He was not the kind, gentle old man that a little girl could trust or admire. He was an alcoholic, a rapist and a child molestor. And, I felt angry, bitter, violated, dirty, guilty, vengeful, and afraid. I was glad when he died but his abuse lived on for many more years in my mind.

"One night I awoke from a restless sleep to face him and tell him how I really felt. He just looked at me with that sinister grin and reached out to touch me one more time. Only this time, I said NO! Never Again! You will never touch 'my little girl' again. I love you, but I love her more and I will not let you abuse her ever again.

"That night I saw my grandpa as the tormented little boy who had always searched for someone to love him. I took him in my arms and held him while he cried away all his years of pain.

"And in the morning when I awoke, hugging my pillow, my grandpa was gone, and he has never returned. Today he is nothing more to me than a vague memory of someone I once thought I knew."

Although I re-established my relationship with my father before he died in 1957, something was always missing. The following entry may offer an explanation:

"When my biological father came to live with us (for one year) when I was twelve I was glad. Then one day on my way out of the bathroom to the bedroom he grabbed the end of my towel, pulled it off, and said, 'Turn around, I want to see my little girl!' Are there any gentle-men? I think I 'dismissed' him then!"

Many women in the group were able to recall very happy and pleasant memories of male figures in their lives as children. Warm, caring men, like my uncle Max, who loved unconditionally. Men whose strength made them feel safe and secure. When I was working on my anger at the men who painfully betrayed me, I began to see the hope on the other side of that anger. Hope kept alive, in part, by positive experiences. And although "ill will" is a very real part of my anger, I know that if I dismiss with ill will, I can't let go of that anger, and I still feel hopeless. I am grateful that I understand this.

I needed to write this step to justify my dismissal of Gust, who sexually molested me for years. When my daughters expressed fear of him, I ordered him out of our lives. Without my knowledge, he had it written in his will that his ashes would be delivered to me when he died. Three years later, a box was delivered by UPS and I learned about his bequest. I kept the urn for several years and then, since I couldn't think of what to do with it, on garbage day I opened it, emptied it into the can, threw the urn in, too, and closed the lid. It just seemed like the only thing to do.

The experience of letting go brings joy to my woman child.

Every woman in the group had been working on this step since the beginning. Somewhere along the way, we started referring to specific steps with pet names (maybe because they don't have numbers). For example, there's the "higher Self" step, the "Ill Will" step, and, of course, the one we were working on, the "Letting Go" step.

When I remember back to the discussions around letting go, I can hear all of us saying at one time or another, "I have let go of _____ (fill in the blank)...several times!" We all agreed "letting go (of him/her/it/that) is hard to do." Over and over we would express our frustration with the fact that just when we were sure we had let go, and had released all reference to the object of our letting go, something would happen that would bring all or some of the attachment flooding back. Letting go takes a lifetime of attention.

Jenny speaks to the struggle of letting go, while Marnie describes her free child:

"Although, at times, I don't enjoy what letting go involves, to get to the point of the freeing experience of letting go, I have to listen to my higher self and truly believe my inner feelings and openly admit my feelings to myself. I then can make an action to let go. I need to remind myself continuously, that yes my feelings are right and feel good for me. This is when I do feel I am treating myself, my woman child, in a warm, comforting, healing way. It takes time and work to care for oneself. But I remember and keep reminding myself, it does matter. You do count, to feel free, not trapped in familiar patterns. You remember the feeling. I know you do: Oh, to watch dust particles just floating by. This is the warmth and joy I return to. I loved it and I still love it; to lie in a pile of hay, peaceful." (Jenny)

"The freeing experience of letting go brings joyous healing to my woman child. My woman child is a favorite part of me. Every thing is ok to her and she is ok to everyone. She moves and breathes and flexes, she fills and breathes and sparkles with life. Assumes no dark motive, is as uncomplicated as the sparrows, doing what she needs to do, not encumbered by the past or weighted by the future. She floats like a leaf and smiles at the sky.

"Ah, to float like a leaf. I stretch my arms and legs and throw back my head and float in the air, and land in a cool stream, soft, gentle, turning, bobbing, I belong right here and wherever I come to rest, I belong also for I am part of this planet, leaves and water and birds are part of my molecules. I am one with the earth." (Marnie)

Linda stimulated our thinking about what not letting go does to our minds and bodies:

"Letting go is so important to my good health. I find it almost impossible to spread my wings and fly free when I am tied down by anger, resentment or unhappy relationships.

"I remember how freeing it was for me when I finally made up my mind to let go of my unhappy marriage. I knew that it was dying and still I kept trying to save it. I just couldn't admit that it was time to move on and let it die with dignity.

"A few months later, I was on my own in 'my' apartment and it felt great. I had lunch with a friend and she said, 'You look great. Have you been on a diet?' She was worried about whether I was eating. I assured her that I was fine and even though I usually wage a constant battle with my bulge, I hadn't even noticed that I was losing weight. I was just busy and I was eating the foods that I liked, and perhaps that was healthier for me.

"Now I know that it was the sense of power that I felt, when I finally decided to let go of the marriage, that enabled me to feel happy and live healthier. It really is a freeing and empowering process for me."

My own entry reveals my feelings:

"When I don't 'let go,' my gut is tight and I am a little sad all the time (as crazy as it sounds), even when I'm happy and functioning."

I don't fully understand why I wrote, "Letting go is an attitude toward life." Since then I have been thinking about it—letting go, that is—a lot. Although I am not exactly clear about it yet, I want to share what I have come up with thus far.

It seems to me that letting go starts way before we "take hold." Now I know this doesn't quite make sense for circumstances that are out of our control, but for most situations, I think it does. It's like this:

If I approach my life *in the present* with complete respect for the past, and complete hope for the future, then the events in my present will take their rightful place in my psyche (soul, heart, life, whatever). There will be no long, tangled tentacle-like cancerous growth suffocating my healthy, life-giving energies. Then when, or if, letting go becomes necessary, it will seem like a natural process. There will be pain and grief, but it will be manageable. The letting go becomes the necessary death before the next new birth.

The truck I just bought has one of those funny mirrors on the passenger side that lets you see a wider angle but makes everything seem farther away. I keep looking in the rear view mirror and then in that mirror attempting to understand that my perceptions of the cars in the right lane behind me are not correct, I must *adjust* my perceptions constantly to avoid trouble. Letting go of other distorted perceptions is not as easy.

This step comes out of my experience of letting go of the pain associated with my childhood. By letting go, I became acquainted with that little cross-eyed girl; when I stopped blaming her, when I understood that being illegitimate was not something bad that she had done, when I understood that being called "white trash" didn't make her trash, when I started celebrating her beauty and strength, her street smarts, her passion, her survival skills, her intelligence, her compassion, I fell in love with her and now that she understands that she is lovable, she is at peace.

The healing that comes from this letting go *is* joyous! It makes me fully open to the woman and the child of the present. I love the many meanings that flow when I play with the words in this step: "to my woman, to my child, to my woman-child."

The following quotation is pasted on the mirror of my mind:

> I no longer try to change outer things. They are simply a reflection. I change my inner perception and the outer reveals the beauty so long obscured by my own attitudes. I concentrate on my inner vision and find my outer view transformed. I find myself attuned to the grandeur of life and in unison with the perfect order of the universe. (*The Book of Runes*)

*I
marvel at my strength
and
celebrate
Her
everpresence.*

This week's step is about women's strength. Most of the group agreed that we as women are usually in tune with the strength we see in other women and it wasn't hard for us to celebrate for each other, but we were much more awkward at celebrating or even naming our own strength. The entries from Lin, Alice, Jenny, and Linda show the wide differences in their approaches to this step.

"Sometimes I feel that part of me isn't alive. I realize that I'm hoping someone will come along and help to ignite that spark in me. I could wait a lifetime.

"So, Lin, don't give your power away. It's not about them out there. It's what is within you…there is much to celebrate—starting right now."

"Growth, knowledge, improvement, at peace with my higher power, daring to share myself, liking my own company. I asked—How will I know when I'm getting better? Answer—I will know by looking at the people I surround myself with." (Alice)

"I surprise myself when I listen to me and I get inner strength and motivation to celebrate me. I must know that it's ok, whatever I'm dealing with. I need to take time and allow time, no matter how small the step in healing. One needs to celebrate to gain strength and to believe in herself. Allow time for your strength, then you can believe you. Celebrate your feelings, thoughts, decisions, and actions. It's your right, however you want to celebrate." (Jenny)

"The word marvel seems to stand out in this phrase because it seems to me that I am often surprised and amazed at my strength whether it is physical, intellectual, emotional or spiritual.

"It takes strength in all of these areas to maintain a B+ average as a college student; especially if you consider that I am a 40-year-old, recently divorced mother of 2 teenage daughters. I am also legally blind, poor (financially) and an out lesbian.

"'It ain't easy' being a successful student under these circumstances and I marvel at my courage, stamina, intelligence and focused determination.

"Yea, me!

"Strength! Marvel!

"It takes a lot of strength to let yourself be loved."   (Linda)

For me, recognizing that ever-present strength, and naming it, started where the strength began, in my childhood; my process from then to the present shows up in these entries:

"How am I strong? I don't know!

"I have courage. I have convictions. I keep going even in the face of pain, discomfort and uncertainty."

"I was born in poverty. I've never had much materially, and what I've had has been tenuous—I mean, could be gone in a flash! I always made the most of things. I have always believed I'd get what I needed some way, somehow, and—in the scheme of things—I have great riches. Recognizing that takes strength."

"Children need full uninterrupted attention. When I was a child, I was given peripheral attention. It was never quite satisfying. I developed a constant need to search for that 'missing something.' Yet there was a strength, a growth force that moved me. I am because I am! I am worthy because I exist! I am as strong as the life force that flows through my soul! Therefore, no one needs to tell me I'm ok to make me ok. I start from the premise of ok-ness with my existence— Talk about a head start!!"

"I think I understand 'detachment' now, that ever-present strength always available even in the down times. Even as a very young child, it made it possible for me to detach, to withdraw psychic energy from any situation or person for my own healing. I remember that time when I was 4 years old and my uncle Mike was breaking Grandma's dishes, one by one, and even though I was scared, I was thinking, 'If I was Grandma, I'd stop that crazy nut!' and then I pushed through the kitchen's swing door and went out and played with the dog. I think that with *understanding* and *knowledge,* women can develop at any age the ability to detach."

I
make room for the
poor choices
of
this day,
and
move on.

When the women in our group met this week, we agreed right away that two things are certain. First, everyone makes mistakes—it's human, and second, there is hardly any room in our society for those mistakes. We decided that it is a built-in system for maintaining a certain level of guilt in everyone. This step is a lifesaver to women, since we appear to experience more than our share of guilt.

In the group, we discussed the workplace, and found that in large institutions and organizations the consequences of this guilt system show up every day: scapegoating, blaming others, covering up, actually being glad someone else was caught instead of us. We decided that all these situations work together to keep employees mistrustful of each other and under enormous stress. I found this to be true in nursing, as is probably true in other occupations which have their own sets of job-related stresses. Subtly encouraging employees to reject or criticize human frailties in themselves and their co-workers is an unnecessary stress. Therefore, since we cannot depend on our society to make room for human error, the women in the group agreed that we must make room for mistakes in ourselves and in others. We decided it was imperative to our healing. Alice and Jenny's entries show their struggle with self acceptance:

"I have a problem committing my thoughts and feelings to paper. It's a permanent record that could be used against me in a future situation and I have a real problem with that. Maybe I could write short stories of my life? Vignettes using a pseudonym. Maybe!! What a way to develop a journal." (Alice)

o 126

"This step is hard for me. I'm a perfectionist, which likes things so-so. I don't want to even admit that I'm so-so. But I know I'm this way. The colors of the rainbow sometimes scare me. I've believed things were this way or that way. However, in my mind and heart I know this is very restricting to my creative part. And it sets me up for failure. When I know, yes, I will make mistakes, why do I believe I won't? Where is this coming from? Allowing myself room for poor choices allows me to be more relaxed with myself, more real, and more creative energy surrounds me. It will get better and I will move on. Trusting my inner voice, the inner woman child. She knows mistakes are made and poor choices happened and she wakes up the next morning and has learned and doesn't forget but is not concentrating on all the bad. She starts out each bright day to seek the colors of the rainbow."   (Jenny)

After I reread the following journal entries I knew I needed to write this step.

"Making room for mistakes in my everyday life, accepting the fact that I will not be able to choose the 'best' every time, takes balance. That's what's missing, balance, that's where my struggle is! I either make a poor choice impulsively and on purpose and call myself 'human' (as an excuse) or I knock myself upside the head and call myself 'stupid.' There is no balance—I am not growing."

"There is growth and I see myself changing when I accept my humanness, frailties and all and still have self-love. That is the balance: self-acceptance and self-love."

One of my favorite Lily Tomlin characters is Edith Ann (age 5). She is completely at home with her humanness and without a doubt loves herself. I read somewhere, in a Marlo Thomas book I think, that Edith Ann likes to go to Sears and pretend she's lost (when she's lonely) so they will call her name over the loudspeaker. She said, "Sears cares about me even though I buy most of my clothes at J.C. Penney's." I would like to hear my name being called when I feel lonely too! ("And that's the truth.")

Compassionately,
I
share
the
peace
that
comes from touching
the
woman within.

After a lively discussion, stimulated by the step for this week, we were able to ferret out the instances in our lives when the societal stereotypes of women and the expected roles women play had influenced our choices.

We talked about the common experience of "giving" energy to men and children and "getting" energy from other women, usually one on one, from mothers, sisters, neighbors, or best friends.

However, we were also well aware of the isolation women experience. The isolation is due, in part, to the mistrust of other women generated by stereotypes. We also named the lack of experiences in group participation there is for women of all ages. It seemed to us that society encourages women to prepare to be with a man and be a homemaker, which does not require team skills. Men, on the other hand, have ample opportunity to develop the degree of trust necessary to succeed in their groups. For some women, severe isolation came from lack of access to family due to either geography or poor communication. The value of groups of women, like this Thirteen Step group, is that here women learn to cooperate and share strength, rather than to compete for control over the group.

Linda, Alice, and Jenny's entries show where they were in their process with this step:

"Does peace come from touching the woman within? This morning I was so upset because I felt like a fish out of water at my field placement. 'They seem to be happy that I'm there, but I want to contribute something.' Neither of us knows what

I'm supposed to be doing there and I feel like I'm lost in a maze looking for a place to fit in.

"As I talked to my best friend I realized that the child within is scared and the woman within needed to say it's ok! Observing is as important as producing at this point. And I took time to softly say to myself: Be gentle with yourself.

"It's hard for me not to have everything totally organized and under my control. In the past that was my way of coping with fear. It also caused tremendous stress and anxiety for me and I don't want that anymore.

"So, today, I have decided to let go of some of the control and allow myself to produce less than 150%. I will be compassionate with myself and share what I can."   (Linda)

"As I get in touch with myself I am more aware of me and my priorities. I try to share this with others. Not always successful."   (Alice)

"After I listen to my inner voice, give her (me) time, allow her time to celebrate my decisions, and actions and to feel good about all. I then can say, to myself, I have compassion towards me. I have touched the inner me, listened to me and feel connected and strong."   (Jenny)

The following entries from my journals reveal some of my early confusion and lack of knowledge about myself. They also show that I was on my way just by naming my feelings.

"I understood at a very early age that as a female my energy and time would be spent on doing for others. I would be what others wanted me to be. I would be defined by others and be identified in relation to others. When I realized that my healing would come from going within I panicked and felt empty."

"Yes, it is true I did spend many years being what others wanted, doing for others, being identified in relation to others. When I realized healing comes from going within I did panic and it was dark inside, my thoughts were so mixed up and confused. I just did not know what to do! I felt like a phony. I wanted someone, anyone to tell me what to do! That was because that's all I had ever known. I had to push through this frightening time and find out what I wanted, set out to get it and believe I deserved it!"

"I think all women share a common pain. Old, young, poor, rich, handicapped or not, of color or not, self-educated or not, lesbian, married, single, with or without children. Being female in a society that controls what I do but refuses to celebrate who I am is painful!"

The pain I experience as a woman does not come from accepting or rejecting society's dictated roles. Most of what I have done in my life has been "traditionally" female and positive. My pain comes from being denied space, skills, and the right to replenish myself. I see no vehicles in society for me or other women to nurture and care for ourselves. Our healing takes longer because we are busy constructing the vehicles.

One conclusion our discussion led us to this week was that sharing is not just "a nice thing to do" but is one of those terrifying risks so necessary to our healing. I wrote the following after that meeting:

"In college I read a book by Sidney Jouard called *Transparent Self.* I have heard the quote about being 'true unto our own selves,' but this author contends that to validate our true selves we must be 'true' unto another person. That is so true for me, when I am 'true to only myself' and keep it a secret, I spend little energy dealing with it. (As I have done with my secret journals buried in the back of the filing cabinet.)

However, when I share with one other person it is impossible for me to ignore my growth. I have to move!...that simple risk leads to growth."

"When I make a personal trip within, I make life-sustaining discoveries. These discoveries most certainly pertain to everyone in some life-affirming way."

At the risk of sounding "so heavenly minded that I am no earthly good," I would like to share a little of my definition of compassion. Compassion describes that connection, that bond or familiarity that comes when that part of me (my Soul?) connects with that certain part of anything else that is living, and there is nothing else to do but to celebrate our membership in the universal family. It has happened for me many times, when I looked into the eyes of my new puppy, at a sunset, down into Mother Earth's womb, the Grand Canyon, and when I held the hand of a dying patient.

All women are beautiful, intelligent, strong, and powerful, and that includes me!

We completed the first cycle of Thirteen Steps with this step. At that point some of us chose to leave the group, and others of us wanted to "circle" again.

Understanding our own beauty and abilities and celebrating them was very difficult. Self-validation and affirmation were not at all familiar to any of us. Therefore, I suggested the following exercise, remembering that as a group and as individual women we had clearly seen the strength in each other. I had each woman repeat the step and then replace the word *me* with the name of any woman of her choice. We circled several times, inserting grandmothers, mothers (not easy for some), friends, authors who had touched our lives, and even women who had hurt us or with whom we were at odds. It was an emotional exercise, an experiential one that symbolized the breaking away from uncertainty and distorted, inaccurate definitions of who we are as women. In their place was the simple truth: "the universe don't make no junk!" Two of my entries, and those of Alice and Jenny, reflect our time together, our growth, and our new beginnings:

"I have lived by male-defined ideas of my beauty for too long. I will no longer ask someone else to validate my beauty."

"The oyster takes the tiny irritating grain of sand, which enters its life uninvited and calmly surrounds it to form a beautiful pearl. Women everywhere continue to surround the uninvited irritants in their lives with gentle woman's strength and give the world an endless variety of gems to be treasured.

"Chronic physical pain is an uninvited irritant in my life. Would that I could see the gem I am forming by surrounding it with my woman's strength. I'm trying...I'm trying...."

"Watching this group come together, seeing the place the women were in, in the beginning, observing the working of the steps and the solutions or paths followed on the journey, have shown great growth and strides in personal and emotional development. This is the proof of this step. To see this marvelous transformation. All women in the group are a living proof of this truth. All women *are* beautiful, intelligent, strong, and powerful and to my wonderment, this *does* include me!

"This is not to say we have reached our destination. We are all on the journey of life and must grow and develop or wither and dry up. We all must eventually die in this lifetime. It's the journey and our companions that are important.

"Thank you, you all hold a special place in my heart. If you must leave, go with my love and best wishes. Otherwise, I look forward to the next growth period with you."   (Alice)

"I do believe this: that all women are strong, are intelligent, are beautiful and hold a power that if and when joined, we have the abilities to end judgmental attitudes, oppressions, gain energies and give energies, care, understand.... We all are alive. And we need to believe these things about ourselves, instead of believing we are not these things. For I believe we are the earth's strength, the ones with peace and healing energies. Don't you believe in yourself? I'm allowing myself to believe these things. I have this right. Be good to yourself: I'm trying to.

"I am growing and learning about myself and encountering many new ideas and thoughts and finally after many years allowing myself to listen to me.

"Once again, thank you Swan, Linda, Marnie, Alice, Lin, and the other women in the group. I'll never forget our energies; they're alive and growing—a circle of warmth and strength. I'm so appreciative that I had the courage within myself to go to that first meeting. It has started."   (Jenny)

Many of my philosophies have come through a movement called "re-evaluation counseling." Many co-counselors will probably recognize these theories throughout this book. The founder's son, Tim Jackins, said, "Co-counseling is an approximation of a natural process." Well, that is what *Thirteen Steps: An Empowerment Process for Women* is, in a manner of speaking. It is *my* approximation of a natural healing process, especially for women.

I get a wonderful feeling when I think of groups of women all over the world creating safe spaces to share their healing with one another. I hope there will be "Thirteen Step sisters" (I am reclaiming stepsister here) everywhere, and that "Thirteen Step sistering" will become a common practice. As Sophia of *Golden Girls* might say, "Picture it, 1999, the U. S. of A., Hackensack, New Jersey. Two women meet at a dentist's office. One says, 'I used to cancel my appointments with the dentist, compulsively finding excuses to avoid my fear.' The other answers, 'I know what you mean. I would have two or three beers before I could make myself keep my appointment, but now I talk my feelings over with a friend, and sometimes I ask her to come along with me. Thanks for telling me that. I've enjoyed sharing with you.'"

What fun! Dreaming about women on planet earth finding healing in everyday places: individual women using the Thirteen Steps to go within; pairs of women becoming Thirteen Step sisters and regularly meeting to empower each other by sharing; groups of women forming safe spaces in a world with few for women. And just the other day, a friend called about using the Thirteen Steps with a client in her counseling practice.

I've also been thinking about a workshop/seminar setting. Why not? The possibilities are endless, as varied as each of you.

Angela Lansbury said that she is most grateful for the opportunity to 'play' to so many people; it's a wonderful 'coup,' she says, to be able to share what one has created. She also said that most of us have something we want to share with the world and never get the opportunity. I know just what she means. I am so grateful to have the opportunity to share my thoughts and feelings in this book.

Since I see this healing as a continuing process, it would be a joy to me to hear from any woman who would be inspired to write and share with Alice, Jenny, Lin, Linda, and all the rest of us your experience with this work of love. You can write to us any time at Spinsters/Aunt Lute. It is important to me that women who read *Thirteen Steps* understand that in no way am I suggesting that my approximation of this healing process is a new idea that I have discovered, nor do I think that it is the only right answer for anyone. I encourage you, the reader, to take what I have shared and use it in any way that works for you. Then when you share with other women, you will be a part of that entire circle of women around the world whose healing hands are circling Mother Earth, allowing all our healing energies to caress Her with love.

When I was a woman-child no one told me that the universe celebrates my woman beauty without reservation. No one told me that I would cycle with the moon when I bled and that my ovaries would shelter the seeds of life as the earth does. Therefore, I had reservations about my self which came from what I *was* told. I was told that lunacy is crazy and the full moon is to be suspected. I was told that 13 was unlucky and to be avoided. I was told to trust that the best place to develop and test instruments of destruction was in the belly of the earth.

So now, I am a grown woman, and this very moment I reclaim lunacy as an affirmation of my beauty as female and every full moon will be my reminder. I reclaim the number 13 (the number of months in the lunar calendar) and every time I see it I will be reminded of the powerful cycling women all over the world (as well as the young women who will and the old women who have). I reclaim Mother Earth, as her trees, flowers, food, rivers, and lakes call to mind my partnership with Her in the ongoing flow of life—I reclaim my Self!!

○ Afterword

Vicki Noble's *Motherpeace: A Way to the Goddess through Myth, Art, and Tarot* has been invaluable to me in my process. But not until I was preparing *Thirteen Steps* for publication did I fully understand the exciting relevance of Vicki's interpretation of numerology to my conception of harmony. In attempting to present the Thirteen Steps as circular rather than hierarchical, I had eliminated the familiar numbering. While reading through the steps, I became concerned about the number of words in each step, because I felt that one had too many words. I counted the words in that step, and there were 17. Since $1 + 7 = 8$, I wondered what Vicki Noble had to say about the number 8.

> Eight is a number of change and inspiration. The eights all represent a change of mood from what has gone before and an entering into some new phase that comes directly out of past experience. ...[Eights] signify movement and new direction. They are definite and external in quality (p. 182–3).

Since the step I had been concerned about was in the middle of the Thirteen Steps, this led me to go back and look at the steps that had come before and count the number of words in them. I was elated at what I discovered. A whole new way of thinking about things opened up before me. Here is what I found.

At the beginning, I had written two steps with 16 words in each. $1 + 6 = 7$. Vicki Noble says that

> Sevens are about inner work, accomplishments on the inner planes, and self-reflection. ...Usually, Sevens concern an inner process of some kind. Something is happening, but one may not be able to see it... (p. 178).

This is what these two steps actually do reflect. This is exactly what they are—inner work.

Next comes a step with 15 words. $1 + 5 = 6$. Vicki's comments about 6 excited me:

> The Sixes are full and expressive, a peak number, always expansive and positive in some way. Six represents exuberance or triumph, being on top of things. Like the sun sitting at the center of the solar system, Six...radiates out in every direction saying "yes!" Six represents a moment of decisive action or a climax of some sort, a moment of glory (p. 175).

How true! Have you ever taken the time to go within, clear your mind, and then make a wise and concise decision? All your being says "Yes!"

The next step contains 14 words. $1 + 4 = 5$.

> Fives are traditionally the number of struggle and conflict, signifying change and some sort of break. ...Because change seems to frighten us, and a break doubly so, the fives have a fearful effect on us. What is important to remember is that destruction is necessary before we can change... (p. 172).

Don't panic—change involves struggle, and sometimes a 'death,' but our own creative energy moves us through it!

The process continued. The next step has 9 words, and 9 is the number of completion.

> Nines, because they are the final single digits of our number system, represent completion and finality. They are the culmination, the summing up of the sequence of numbers (p. 185).

It appears to me that when inner work and struggle are completed, we are preparing ourselves for change.

The next two steps represent the number 8, the number for change, according to Vicki Noble.

Then comes a step with 13 words. $1 + 3 = 4$. The number 4 indicates stability in Vicki's interpretation.

> Representing the four directions, the Fours...form a square or a cross, figures that bring order along with a sense of limitation. Four signifies the weighty element of physical matter and encloses the personality. ...This creates a separation between inner and outer, a space where something special can occur (p. 168).

From here the steps move to balance ("receptivity and magnetism...twos signify polarity and balance between opposites" [p. 161]) and then to completion and stability again.

Completing the cycle are two steps with 12 words each. $1 + 2 = 3$, which represents synthesis:

> Synthesizing the active and passive...a *triangle* that signifies harmony and flow (p. 164). (Italics mine)

Following the order in which they were originally written, the Thirteen Steps emerge in this way:

7—inner work (two steps)
6—exuberance
5—struggle
9—completion
8—change (two steps)
4—stability
2—balance

9—completion
4—stability
3—synthesis (two steps)

Circularly thinking, if a woman chose to start with inner work, move to exuberance, struggle, completion, and change, then to stability, balance, completion, and stability, around to synthesis, she would be ready to circle again.

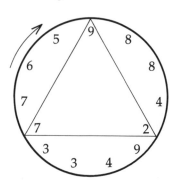

However, by keeping a record of the order she is following when using the Thirteen Steps, a woman can create her own numerical healing circle representing her own personal healing process, by filling in (replacing) her personal sequence of numbers.

This process is beautifully described here by Marnie:

"How does it feel to be whole? A circle with gaps, slowly moving, even, measured, smooth, clear from beginning to beginning and past the beginning again. To be healed, to heal is to continue past the beginning in a circle over and over again, pulling in the new, making what *is* stronger and firmer, not increasing the speed, only stronger and firmer...."

Bonita L. Swan was born in Chicago, Illinois on March 28, 1934. She lived with her single, handicapped mother in Chicago's first housing project (Jane Addams). She also spent many rewarding hours at the settlement house founded by Jane Addams and is proud to be a former Hull House kid.

Swan is dyslexic and an avid reader, describing herself as "a self-taught student of life." This pattern began at age 13, when she taught herself to read because her teachers did not know how to teach the way she learns.

Four years later, in 1952, she graduated from high school and then married. For the next several years her focus was on her two daughters and three sons.

In the late 1960s, she returned to school and received an associate degree in Nursing from Rock Valley College, Rockford, Illinois. After several years in medical-surgical nursing and a divorce in 1976, she decided to focus on the psychiatic nursing of children. She believes they are society's most valuable natural resource. Her specialty eventually became chemically dependent teens.

No longer able to meet the physical demands of nursing, due to a spinal injury and arthritis, Swan is retired and lives in Phoenix, Arizona.

Thirteen Steps: An Empowerment Process for Women is her first book and candidly presents the continuing process of her healing integration.

▣ spinsters book company

Spinsters Book Company was founded in 1978 to produce vital books for diverse women's communities. In 1986 we merged with Aunt Lute Books to become Spinsters/Aunt Lute. In 1990, the Aunt Lute Foundation became an independent non-profit publishing program.

Spinsters is committed to publishing works outside the scope of mainstream commercial publishers: books that not only name crucial issues in women's lives, but more importantly encourage change and growth; books that help to make the best in our lives more possible. We sponsor an annual Lesbian Fiction Contest for the best lesbian novel each year. And we are particularly interested in creative works by lesbians.

If you would like to know about other books we produce, or our Fiction Contest, write or phone us for a free catalogue. You can buy books directly from us. We can also supply you with the name of a bookstore closest to you that stocks our books. We accept phone orders with Visa or MasterCard.

Spinsters Book Company
P.O. Box 410687
San Francisco, CA 94141
415-558-9586